You're the Best!

Reflections on the Life of Houston Nutt

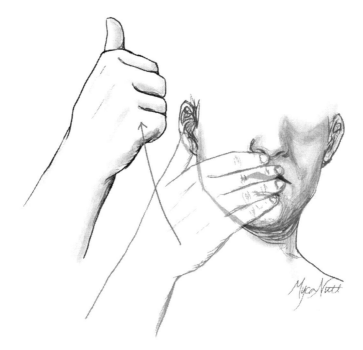

YOU'RE THE BEST!
Drawing by Myca Nutt, granddaughter

Emogene Dickey Nutt

CROSSBOOKS

CrossBooks™
A Division of LifeWay
One LifeWay Plaza
Nashville, TN 37234
www.crossbooks.com
Phone: 1-866-768-9010

Scripture taken from the New King James Version. Copyright 1979, 1980, 1982 by Thomas Nelson, inc. Used by permission. All rights reserved.

Scriptures taken from the Holy Bible, New International Version®, NIV®. Copyright © 1973, 1978, 1984, 2011 by Biblica, Inc.™ Used by permission of Zondervan. All rights reserved worldwide. www.zondervan.com The "NIV" and "New International Version" are trademarks registered in the United States Patent and Trademark Office by Biblica, Inc.™ All rights reserved.

Scripture taken from the New Century Version. Copyright © 2005 by Thomas Nelson, Inc. Used by permission. All rights reserved.

First published by CrossBooks 9/2/2014

ISBN: 978-1-4627-3465-8 (sc)
ISBN: 978-1-4627-3464-1 (hc)
ISBN: 978-1-4627-3466-5 (e)

Library of Congress Control Number: 2014901197

Printed in the United States of America.

This book is printed on acid-free paper.

Any people depicted in stock imagery provided by Thinkstock are models, and such images are being used for illustrative purposes only. Certain stock imagery © Thinkstock.

DEDICATIONS

To the memory
of
Houston Nutt, Sr.,

To our sons: Houston Dale, Dickey, Danny, and Dennis,

To our daughters-in-law: Diana, Cathy, Carla and Vicki, and

To our grandchildren: Houston III, twins Hanna and Hailey, and Haven; Logan, Luke, Lexis; Dallas, triplets Ashley, Brenna, and Caylan; and twins Myca and Macy, giving them a glimpse of the past—interwoven with Deafness.

SPECIAL THANKS

To Janis Scott, who brought me a three-ring notebook
filled with lined paper and suggested topics—
otherwise, I might have never started this book,

To Sheila Spratlin, who gave me encouragement
and who initially typed this manuscript, and

To Bill and Vera Downs: for their work as editors
in preparing the manuscript for publication.

CONTENTS

PROLOGUE. ix

INTRODUCTION. xi

CHAPTER 1   Life in the '30s 1

CHAPTER 2   Houston's Family. 5

CHAPTER 3   Houston's Early Childhood .17

CHAPTER 4   Houston's College Days 39

CHAPTER 5   Introduction To Family And ASD 51

CHAPTER 6   Houston Begins Coaching At ASD. 65

CHAPTER 7   Player/Coach 83

CHAPTER 8   The Bennie Fuller Era; 1965-1971 95

CHAPTER 9   Houston's Last Games and Retirement 105

CHAPTER 10   Houston's Closing Chapter .119

CHAPTER 11   Houston Remembered 129

CHAPTER 12   Carrying on a Legacy 139

EPILOGUE. 227

APPENDIX 1   Reasonable Tax 229

APPENDIX 2   "The Bear" 230

APPENDIX 3   Samuel Fordyce 231

APPENDIX 4   Fordyce 232

APPENDIX 5   Great-Grandfather 233

APPENDIX 6   Vocational Training For The Deaf 235

APPENDIX 7   Martha's Vineyard. 236

APPENDIX 8   Historical Heroes In Deaf Education. 237

APPENDIX 9   Fordyce Basketball 1949-50. 239

APPENDIX 10   Legendary Coaches. 240

APPENDIX 11   The Outlook For 1951-52 242

APPENDIX 12   A Bit Of History. 244

APPENDIX 13   Coaches Winning 20 Games Or More. 246

APPENDIX 14   Bennie Fuller's High School Statistics 247

APPENDIX 15   A House Resolution 248

PROLOGUE

I guess I knew one day I would write a book about Houston. It is about more than being born to deaf parents, being raised in a deaf environment where all of his siblings were either totally or partially deaf or even communicating by sign language. It is about more than having played for two legendry coaches ... it is about the American Dream!

Things in Houston's life, which could have been a detriment to some, were handled with ease, according to Jack Gresham, superintendent of Fordyce High School.

Houston set high goals for himself in athletics and his dream was to grow up and make life better for deaf people. In addition to this dream, he had an unbelievable passion for basketball.

He pulled himself up by his own bootstraps—some would say "disadvantaged" bootstraps—and literally hitchhiked his way to the very top in the realm of basketball, never losing sight of his little-boy dream.

> *"So I will very gladly spend for you everything I have and expend myself as well"* (II Corinthians 12:15 - NIV).

His journey had its beginning by sharing his hometown with a lifelong friend—the famous Paul "Bear" Bryant, who was born in the little community of Moro Bottom. In a neighboring town, his biggest football rival was David Pryor, who one day would become the governor of Arkansas and our U. S. Senator.

Houston's dedication and hard work earned him a college education and he lived out his dream of coaching basketball and working with the deaf at the Arkansas School for the Deaf in Little Rock, Ark.

He received just about every honor there was to receive, including being inducted into the Arkansas Sports Hall of Fame; however, his greatest honor was as a father to his four sons, who incidentally are carrying on his legacy.

During those 49 years, while at work and in retirement, acquaintances and friends were constantly telling Houston he should write a book. However, while he was coaching, there was never time. In retirement, our sons were coaching and there were games far and near. Then thirteen grandchildren came along, each one playing some kind of game. Our time was totally consumed.

Soon after Houston had passed away, Janis Scott who, I believe, God so graciously placed in our neighborhood, brought me a loose-leaf notebook complete with lined paper and suggested topics: "You're the Best," "Houston Meets Future Wife," "Coach at ASD," "A Phenomenal Player," etc., etc. It could no longer be postponed. It was the right time to start writing this book.

"To everything there is a season, and a time to every purpose under the heaven:" (Ecclesiastes 3:1 - KJV).

I went to the basement and dragged out an old plastic bag that contained a musty, smelly scrapbook bulging open with pages, plus many loose pages. There were articles on every game since 1956— Deaf School Games, Little Rock Silents Games, Benefit Games, Pee Wee Games, Milan, Italy Games and much, much more.

The first two years after Houston's "home-going," every spare moment was spent gathering information and writing. I will admit it was an exhilarating experience, as well as a therapeutic one. I hope you will enjoy reading it as much as I enjoyed writing it.

INTRODUCTION

There is no simple definition for deaf culture; in fact, it is complex.

It seems that in today's world, American Sign Language (ASL) and deaf culture go hand in hand. In fact, it is true the deaf have a very special language and culture.

When we came to the Arkansas School for the Deaf in 1956, the language was not referred to as ASL. It was called sign language and, seeing it for the first time, I was totally spellbound! I was intrigued and I wanted to learn that language. As for deaf culture, it was never a topic of discussion nor was it ever mentioned in any of my deaf education classes; therefore, it is a relatively new concept. Today, deaf culture is all the talk. Everyone wants to know about it and who is part of it.

It may not be easily recognized, but you will not be in a deaf community long before you experience it, as I have explained in this book. I am referring to their conversation, which may be very blunt, straightforward and to the point.

One of the complexities of deaf culture is that being deaf does not mean you are a part of the deaf culture. For example, people who lose their hearing from illnesses, or deaf children who are born to hearing parents, often have not been privileged to sign language or the knowledge that makes up the deaf culture. Most do acquire the language and culture later in life; however, their acceptance into deaf culture partially depends on their skill in the language.

Then there are people, like my husband, Houston Sr., born into deaf culture, inheriting the language along with the culture, and they take much pride in this. If you are not born into this culture, the next best way to learn about it is to live in the residential dormitory at a school for the deaf.

When we came to ASD in the 50s, the school for the most part was staffed with deaf people who attended the school at one time, and the children and others learned the language from the adults and the other students. The children living in the dorm were observing attitudes, prejudices, engaging in social behaviors and participating in games and sports, which are all part of deaf culture. The deaf children were submerged in this language and culture all of their school days and it was passed down from generation to generation.

> **"Arguments Raised Against the Continuance of the Deaf Culture:** It is acknowledged by those in the Deaf community that special clubs and residential schools for the Deaf, historically the main conduits through which the culture has been passed on from generation to generation, no longer hold that position. The mistake is to assume that the diminishing influence of these two institutions foretells the eventual disappearance of Deaf culture. Rather, what the demise of clubs and residential schools suggest, particularly in light of Deaf history, is that the socioeconomic status of the Deaf has been catapulted out of its isolated and exclusionary position of old and, in response, the new generation is compelled to find new ways of expressing and transmitting its cultural identity." – Quote in part from *The Future of the Deaf Culture*, by Paul W. Ogden, Ph.D. and Keila M. Classen, M. A. p. 65.

We have come from times when the deaf were embarrassed to be seen signing in public to a time when every public event has an interpreter. The deaf clubs, once necessary not only for social gatherings, but to gain information, are now largely replaced by Internet and phone technology.

As mentioned in *The Future of the Deaf Culture,* "... the new generation is compelled to find new ways of expressing and transmitting its cultural identity." And I believe they will in their revolutionary world of the 21st century.

CHAPTER 1

LIFE IN THE '30S

This story has its beginning in the early '30s and is best defined by the Great Depression, a time when electricity and plain running water in the home were nearly impossible.

Life in this era would be shocking and in some ways incomprehensible, especially for our grandchildren who live in a digital world of wireless phones, texting, high-definition television and much more.

> "With the stock-market crash of 29 October, 1929, and the resulting Great Depression, Arkansas, a state that ranked forty-sixth in per capita income, sank for the next decade into a quagmire of unemployment, bankruptcy, farm foreclosures, and dire poverty." - *Governors of Arkansas*, p. 177.

This was a tough time in our history and certainly the lowest point in the Great Depression. Nevertheless, the Governor of Arkansas, Harvey Parnell (1928-1933), forged ahead with his favorite projects—one of which was a new school for deaf children in Little Rock, which was accomplished by a "reasonable tax." (See Appendix 1.)

Parnell Hall

AN INTERESTING TURN OF EVENTS

Two and a half decades later, Houston and I would come on the scene and spend the next 30-plus years of our lives at the Arkansas School for the Deaf. In fact, most of our waking hours would be spent in that building, which was Parnell Hall. It was very much a part of our lives. All of Houston's practices and home games were played in that gymnasium, his second home and his pride and joy. And I taught 28 of my 31 years in that very building.

After seven decades, the classrooms are still in use and graduating seniors continue to walk across the stage on graduation day. The gymnasium was outgrown in the '70s, but is used for a multitude of purposes today. It is located on ASD campus overlooking Markham Street. It was an amazing building in those days and still is.

A HANDSOME LITTLE TOWN

Those of you who did not grow up during the Great Depression have at least heard about the hardships, but have you heard about the famous little town of Fordyce, located in Dallas County, Ark.? It was often referred to as a "handsome little town," and is located just about

75 miles south of Little Rock and the population was approximately 4,000 in the early '30s. One of the reasons this little town is famous is that it is the hometown of Coach "Bear" Bryant. (See Appendix 2.)

Fordyce at that time was not only a distinguished little town but was a thriving one because of the two major railroads, the Georgia Pacific from the east and the Union Pacific from the west. The town was named for Samuel Fordyce, who was quite an extraordinary man. (See Appendix 3.)

The town's most celebrated traditional attraction was, and still is, the Fordyce on the Cotton Belt Festival, symbolizing the importance of the early railroads.

Fordyce was the first town in the state to have a football team that was organized in 1904 by a former New Yorker, Tom Meddick. (See Appendix 4.)

The people with whom I had the opportunity to visit are very proud to call Fordyce their hometown and agree it is a "handsome little town."

Ab Nutt family

May Nutt   *Ab Nutt*

CHAPTER 2

HOUSTON'S FAMILY

Mr. and Mrs. Ab Nutt were among the residents of this handsome little town of Fordyce. Most would remember this family because of their deafness but they were also a respected family.

Houston's mother, May, was a dedicated mother and housewife. In addition to raising her six children, she also raised her brother's daughter, Margie, from infancy. She raised her large family in a small, unpainted frame house and all the household chores were done without electricity or indoor plumbing.

May never left her home for shopping or even an errand. If anything was needed from the grocery store or department store, either her husband or one of the children would get it for her and that included everything she wore. That's how it was when I became part of the family and that practice continued throughout her life.

May was very protective of her children and was especially fearful of water. She never allowed her children to go near rivers, lakes or ponds. She never saw any of her sons play ball outside the back yard. The idea of valuable lessons learned from playing ball or that those lessons run parallel to life were never thoughts of hers. She knew it was something the boys loved very much, but never in her wildest thoughts could she imagine that a college education could be earned by playing ball.

May lost her hearing as a young adult from taking too much quinine, which was a medicine used in those days for fevers and chills. Her interests were totally family and home. She died in the spring of 1980 at 80 years of age, because of failing health.

Houston's father, Ab, was one of 12 children: Franklin, Rosie, Nan, Burrell, Emmaline, Charles, Laura, Beatrice (Beadie), Albert (Ab), Jacob, Bethany, and Floyd. All of them made it to adulthood and well beyond. That was remarkable considering there were no antibiotics, and it was near impossible to see a doctor. Their means of transportation were horseback and wagon.

The story of how Ab's grandfather, Benjamin Franklin Nutt, who died at the end of a hangman's rope, is told in Appendix 5.

Ab attended the deaf school, but he had to quit school at a very early age to help his father on the farm with the crops and livestock. Although Ab was deaf, he had a lot of speech and could talk quite well, I'm told.

Ab would not only be remembered by his deafness but by his work ethic. He worked from sunup to sundown in spite of his circumstances. He never used his deafness as an excuse nor did he ever draw a supplement check.

Remember, at this time in our history, deaf people were looked upon as severely handicapped and set apart from the hearing world. The only work available to them was low-skilled, manual-labor jobs, if anything at all. Ab also knew he had to try twice as hard even to have an opportunity to get a job and had to prove he was capable of doing it.

He did anything he could to provide a living for his family. He hauled wood in addition to truck farming, which was growing all kinds of vegetables and watermelons. The vegetables were canned and preserved for winter months. He also butchered hogs and cows for the Kilgore Hotel and Restaurant in Fordyce—I might add that butchering was a very tough job. They had plenty to eat, but lived on the bare minimum.

IT WAS NOT ALL WORK AND NO PLAY!

At times, Ab played baseball with his brothers and sons on teams sponsored by the local merchants in Fordyce. His niece, Louise, remembers him as the team clown. She recalls that in one particular game Ab showed up wearing overalls, his cap on backwards and his high-top shoes on the wrong feet. He stepped up to the plate in batting position and wiggled his backside. Clyde, his son, who was the pitcher for the opposing team, was so overcome with laughter he couldn't pitch. No one remembers the outcome of that game, of course, only Ab's attire and actions.

He was also the family prankster when the families got together. He would paint his face, wrap up in a sheet, hide and wait. When the kids came out, he would scare them unmercifully. He was also a favorite uncle, according to nieces and nephews, in spite of his teasing or maybe because of it.

I did not have the privilege of knowing Ab before his stroke in 1952. From all accounts, he was a remarkable person and some of his sons inherited his sense of humor.

Three of Ab's brothers, Frank, Burrell and Charles, and one sister, Bethany, were born totally deaf and attended the Arkansas School for the Deaf. The deafness in the family was hereditary. The uncles and aunt married deaf spouses and they lived near each other in the community. They provided for their families and were good citizens. The multi-generational deaf families are referred to as "deaf dynasties."

Deaf born to deaf parents is a source of pride in the deaf community and Houston's family was a living testament to that. They have a better understanding of what it means to be deaf because of their deaf parents and relatives, and their skill in ASL exceeds their deaf peers who were born to hearing parents.

Deaf children born to hearing parents, who have no prior experience with ASL, acquire language differently than those who are born to deaf parents.

Nine out of ten children who are born deaf are born to hearing parents and often times these parents are devastated; whereas, deaf parents having deaf children are very much at peace. These deaf families, or deaf dynasties, were very close and stuck together, as you can imagine. They shared something unique, a culture and a language that belonged only to them.

In their book, *For Hearing People ONLY,* Matthew S. Moore and Linda Levitan wrote:

> "Since so many Deaf parents are fluent Signers, deaf children born into such families begin life with complete immersion in the language of the parents and start school with considerable advantage over deaf children from non-signing hearing families.
>
> "Deaf children of Deaf parents have traditionally been the transmitters of sign language and Deaf culture to their schoolmates; the leaders, the boat-rockers. They tend to grow up with a sense of identity, a pride that many deaf children of hearing parents initially lack."

Ab's deaf brothers learned shoe repair at the deaf school. As shoe cobblers, they were better off than most in providing for their families during the Great Depression days. Charlie was especially gifted as a shoe cobbler and continued in the shoe business throughout his lifetime. (See Appendix 6.)

Bethany completed her work at the deaf school and the preparation for teaching but she never taught. She married a deaf man, Alpha Patterson, who was a teacher for the deaf in California.

Floyd Nutt, the youngest of Ab's siblings, had perfect hearing. His deaf brothers taught him shoe repair. He had a flourishing shoe repair business in Little Rock when Houston and I began our work at the deaf school in 1956. Later years he moved his shop to North Little Rock.

Uncle Floyd was the only uncle Houston had an opportunity to be with in his adult life and memories were precious. He and Houston carried on conversations in sign language and they were particularly proud of that. They reveled in the fact that Aunt Mary and I couldn't understand much of anything that was being said.

Uncle Floyd also took Houston frog gigging, but Houston didn't catch the frogs like everybody else. He caught them with his hands and Uncle Floyd got a thrill out of that.

Floyd served in the U.S. Coast Guard. He was born in January 1904 and passed away in January 1976.

Jake and Bethany Nutt with Bethany and Floyd

Basketball team, Charles Robert Nutt (on right)

Bethany Nutt (second from left – front row) at Deaf School, 1920

A LEGEND IS BORN

"Before I formed you in the womb I knew you, before you were born I set you apart; I appointed you as a prophet to the nation" (Jeremiah 1:5 - NIV).

At a time in our history that will never be forgotten and in a distinguished, even famous little place, a legend was born. One can only imagine the beautiful, brilliant blue sky suspended over Fordyce, Ark. on that morning of October 9, 1930, when Houston Nutt, Sr. was born to Albert "Ab" and May Pennington Nutt.

Houston Sr.

Houston with Mom and Dad

Houston was the fifth child born to this family. The firstborn was a sister, Ludie Bell; four brothers—Fred, Claude (who died at an early age), Clyde, and Houston. There were two children to come after Houston—a brother, Fay, and a sister, Ella Reace. There was also a child who died soon after birth.

Houston looked like a typical little tow-headed boy with blue eyes, a wide forehead and a cowlick; however, there was something that was not quite so typical: He was born into a deep, deaf culture and communicated by sign language.

Sign language was his first language and was very much a part of him—as if woven into every fiber of his physical being. A deaf child born to deaf parents who already uses ASL will grasp this language as naturally as a hearing child picks up spoken language from hearing parents.

Sign language was used exclusively in the home, because of the deafness in the family, and they took pride in this. Houston grew up in a very secure deaf environment, which led him to believe deafness was the norm. He not only had deaf brothers and sisters but deaf parents as well. This placed him in a minority group where, according to national statistics, only 9 to 10 percent of deaf children have deaf parents.

Houston never thought of deafness or the loss of hearing as a handicap or disability. They were all expected to do well and achieve, as did their deaf parents and relatives. The boys were all good athletes, as was the youngest sister. The only thing they couldn't do was hear perfectly and some couldn't hear at all.

SIGN LANGUAGE

This family relied on ASL to communicate, along with half a million other people across our nation. Signs are very old and can be traced all the way back to 18th century France. Approximately two-thirds of today's signs have French origin.

> "ASL has evolved from a blend of Old French Language and what's now called 'Old American Sign Language,' which has been traced to the dialect used in the communities at Martha's Vineyard. (See Appendix 7.)

"Some sort of native sign language was being used well over a century before Laurent Clerc brought French Sign Language to the states in 1817.

"Linguists have only recently begun to pay serious attention to ASL as a language, but ASL has already begun to enrich American culture through theatre, poetry, song, Sign Mime, and storytelling. ASL is a beautiful and expressive language that is finally beginning to get the respect it deserves." - *For Hearing People ONLY*, Matthew S. Moore and Linda Levitan.

The American Sign Language (ASL) has been the topic of controversial research. "In the last 20 years, however, ASL has gained more and more credibility and is now largely recognized as a bona fide language." - *Deaf Education at the Dawn of the 21st Century*, p. 68.

Since this book was written with my grandchildren in mind, I would be remiss not to relate this inspirational story about one of our pioneers in the education of the deaf and one who exemplifies, '...*love your neighbor as yourself*' (Matthew 19:19 – NIV).

Thomas Hopkins Gallaudet, (1787-1851), born in Philadelphia, Pennsylvania, graduated from Yale University with highest honors at 17. He also earned a masters degree from Yale and then later a degree from Andover Theological Seminary in hopes of becoming a minister. However, his plans were put on hold when he met Alice Cogswell, the little girl next door.

Gallaudet noticed she did not play with the other children and he asked his little brother about her. He said, "She can't play, she's 'deaf and dumb.'" (In earlier times, the deaf were referred to as "deaf and dumb.")

Gallaudet started working with her and teaching her names of things. First, he handed her his hat and drew the letters *"HAT"* in the sand. He did this over and over until she understood, and that was the beginning of deaf education in America.

Alice's father, Dr. Cogswell, sent Gallaudet to Europe to study ways to teach deaf children. After observing methods of teaching, Gallaudet persuaded Clerc, a deaf teacher, to return to America with him. The two of them founded the first school for the deaf in Hartford, Connecticut, in 1817.

Originally, the school was called The American Asylum at Hartford for the Deaf and Dumb, and was later changed to The American School for the Deaf.

Thomas Hopkins Gallaudet was a remarkable man who "loved his neighbor as himself," and "whose life and work left an indelible imprint on the American scene." - *Gallaudet, Friend of the Deaf* by Etta De Gering. (See Appendix 8.)

I would encourage everyone to read this and, as you do, keep a box of tissues nearby.

FINGER-SPELLING

Finger spelling is a part of sign language. The letters of the alphabet are formed by different positions of the hand and fingers. It is believed about 8.5 percent of casual signing in ASL is finger spelling. It is also believed that the percentage is higher in older deaf people.

Finger spelling is vital, especially for clarification, such as names, places, titles, or anything in question. As the saying goes, "When in doubt, *SPELL*." The alphabet is also used to spell words that do not have signs and, as mentioned before, is a distinct part of sign language. It is difficult to read and frequently takes years of expressive and receptive practice to become skilled in finger spelling. When I first saw deaf people finger spell, I could not tell when a word ended and the next one began.

When our second son, Dickey, was about three years old, he would spell a word, throw his hand downward to let you know that the word was finished, then begin to spell the next word. This procedure was repeated until he finished the sentence. He felt there was a need to let his viewers know when a word ended and the new one began. I loved it! I felt the same way.

When we came to the deaf school, finger spelling was used extensively, especially in the upper- and middle-school classrooms. During that time, most of our teachers were older people who happened to be deaf and finger-spelled everything.

When finger spelling is mentioned, Mr. Luther Shibley immediately comes to mind. Mr. Shibley was a wonderful teacher, mentor and friend at ASD for more than 50 years. He was deaf and a graduate of Gallaudet College in Washington, D. C. His work ethic and integrity made him a perfect role model with whom the deaf students could identify. He demanded that his students spell each word. Even though a student can sign a word and use it correctly in the sentence, he or she still may not know how to spell that word. His philosophy was, "If you can't spell, you can't write—*SPELL, SPELL, SPELL!*"

The deaf children were definitely privileged to have had Mr. Shibley as their teacher, mentor, and friend.

"A teacher affects eternity; he can never tell where his influence stops." -Henry Brooks Adams.

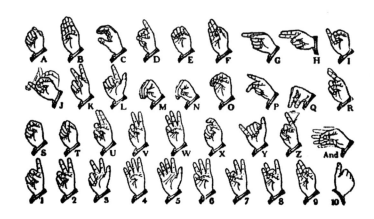

Drawing of the Manual Alphabet

CHAPTER 3

HOUSTON'S EARLY CHILDHOOD

HOUSTON ATTENDS THE DEAF SCHOOL

Houston's Class at Arkansas School for the Deaf in 1939. Houston (on left). Other class members: Betty Sue Beene, Mary Bray, Yvonne Drennan, Rosalyn Jordan, Jack Riley, Wilson Lewis, Billy Whitson, Paul Eastep, Woodrow Harris, Florene Shears and Mrs. L. G. Hinkson, teacher.

When Houston was old enough to go to school, he persuaded his parents to let him attend the Arkansas School for the Deaf. He had two older brothers, Fred and Clyde, who attended the school and he wanted to go to school with them. Hearing tests were not available in those days and the parents really didn't know how much he could or could not hear. Under the circumstances, it seemed to be the natural thing to do.

Although Houston was away at school, he was still in his own comfortable "cocoon," along with two of his siblings, in a safe deaf environment much like the one he knew at home. It couldn't get much better than that—but not for long.

I am not sure how long Houston attended the school before the teachers discovered he had too much hearing to attend the deaf school. Much to his disappointment, he was sent back home to attend the public school in Fordyce, Arkansas. Although he was disappointed at the time, I'm sure he would thank those teachers today, if he could, for sending him to public school.

PUBLIC SCHOOL AND SIGN LANGUAGE

After attending the deaf school, Houston was enrolled in the public school in Fordyce. Now he is thrust into a different world. He not only must adjust to a new school where everyone used the English language, but must adjust to a new world—a hearing world. For the first time, he could not communicate by using sign language. At school, he had to talk to be understood and from that point in his life he actually juggled two worlds.

In the public school he did not have his brothers but, as a consolation, there were cousins whose first language was also sign language. They could say anything they wanted in their native language and no one could understand what they were saying.

There were many stories about those school days in Fordyce. On the playground as well as in the classroom, the bond among those cousins was definitely intact. If there was a problem, the whole clan would be *"up-in-arms." Fights did break out, of course, if their parents were made fun of or called names like "deaf and dumb," or "dummy" because of their deafness.

---

* up-in-arms – ready to fight

As a teacher, I can understand the frustration and problems with the ASL/sign language, especially on test day. Those flying fingers can work ever so discreetly in sharing answers.

Children who are deaf are still the same in one respect:

> *"The heart is deceitful above all things and desperately wicked; who can know it?"* (Jeremiah 17:9, NKJV).

When I first started working with the deaf, I thought because they couldn't hear they were surely partially *CELESTIAL*—if not totally. I was so disappointed when I found out that was not the case.

No, the deaf are not exempt because they can't hear, in spite of what you might think. People who are not familiar with the deaf may be inclined to excuse them! Don't!

By school age, hopefully, integrity was one of their strongest traits even though it may have been learned through sign language, rather than spoken English.

From all reports, including the nature of the "heart," all those children who used sign language and grew up in a deaf culture did very well.

TREASURED CHILDHOOD MEMORIES

Chicken sandwiches - Houston's mom enjoyed telling the story about Houston selling chicken sandwiches. The story went something like this: May, Houston's mother, would boil the chicken, shred it, place it on the bread, drizzle it with Heinz 57, and Houston was in business. He would jump on his bicycle and head to the bus station area to sell the sandwiches. His next stop was the train depot, if there were any sandwiches left. The sandwiches were sold for 25¢ a piece. He would bring the money home, give it to his mother and she would carefully count the money and lock it safely in her trunk. Houston could sell the sandwiches literally faster than his mother could prepare them. I've heard that the money was used to help buy the land on Moro Street in Fordyce, where the family home is today.

As years passed by, that story was told again and again. I always wondered if Houston volunteered to sell the sandwiches or did it come down to: Whom shall I send? And Houston said, "Here am I; send me." None of the other children were ever mentioned in this story. I don't know why I didn't ask and it's too late now.

Houston, his mom, sister and others have related this story to me numerous times and, from all accounts, it was a most memorable and enjoyable experience, as well as profitable.

A ride in dad's wagon - On Saturday mornings Houston and his dad would go pick up the day-old cinnamon rolls from the Kilgore Hotel and be on their way to an area where many African-American families lived. With each visit, Houston's dad gave at least one or two of the youngsters a dip of snuff just to see the reaction on their faces.

After the stunts of mischief and fun, the boys were treated to cinnamon rolls. When the last cinnamon roll was eaten and they said their good-byes, Houston and his dad had quality time riding home in the wagon. Watching his eyes light up as he told the story, it was a treasured time, no doubt. Those times with his dad stayed with him his entire life, as did the idea of helping others less fortunate.

In Houston's retirement, instead of day-old cinnamon rolls, it was barbeque. Quite often he would buy enough barbeque to treat the whole crew at different businesses. However, to my knowledge, he never tried any of his dad's trickery! Next to watching games, especially grandchildren's games, treating someone to barbeque was at the top of his list.

Could those special wagon rides with his dad account for Houston's practice of giving and treating others with generosity?

Off limits! - When Houston was growing up, certain places were off limits and the pool hall was one of them. His father heard that he was spending time in the town pool hall. He walked in one afternoon and there was Houston, watching his uncles play pool. Houston got a "lick" with his dad's horse whip. He got the message real quick—the town pool hall was off limits and, as the story goes, he never darkened those doors again!

Houston's dad, Ab, was of the generation that did not tell his children on a daily basis they were loved; however, they were. The children of that generation didn't have "time out"—instead they got whippings and/or a lick, as in this case. They all made it to adulthood and became good citizens in spite of the way they were disciplined and without being told they were loved on a regular basis.

A GREAT INFLUENCE

Now, you have met that father who worked from sunup to sundown and that mother, the traditional hard-working homemaker doing what it takes to raise her large family. It was a hard life but I never heard them complain. They were proud of their family and their deafness was totally accepted. Perhaps material assets were lacking, but nothing outweighs parental guidance, love and example.

"There is nothing more influential in a child's life than the moral power of quiet example." -William Bennett - *The Book of Virtues.*

Houston realized hard work was an important part of his parents' lives, and he tried to live up to their expectations. Although he did not have to earn a living as they did, he worked hard at what he did. The time and hard work put into training and playing ball gained him a college education and a different path for his life. Houston was proud of his deaf heritage and his parents were definitely a big influence in his life.

"Houston handled his situation with the greatest of ease, which could have been a real challenge or even a hardship," said his high school superintendent, Mr. Jack Gresham. In an Arkansas Democrat-Gazette article, Rex Horne said of Houston, "What some would call a hardship, Houston turned into an opportunity to help others."

OTHER GREAT INFLUENCES

"As iron sharpens iron, so a man sharpens the countenance of his friend" (Proverbs 27:17 – NKJV).

I'm sure many people influenced Houston's life that I do not know about; however, there are a couple of people I do know about, who were very influential during those years at Fordyce.

First, Mr. Jack Gresham, superintendent at Fordyce High School, was a friend and mentor. He not only was a great educator but a good man who took a personal interest in Houston. He said Houston was always in the gym after school and he would go to the gym and shoot baskets with him. They developed a life-long relationship. He kept up with Houston all through college and during his coaching career. When the boys came along, he kept up with them as well. In one of his letters, he wrote, "Then along came his boys to carry the mantle Houston had set at the public schools and colleges and every advancement by these sons carried the Houston brand."

Mr. Gresham was a great influence and Houston loved and appreciated all he did for him. One could say, Mr. Gresham is "... *the salt of the earth ...the light of the world*" (Matthew 5:13,14 – NIV).

The other person who had a great influence on Houston's life was the pastor at First Baptist Church in Fordyce, Arkansas, the Rev. J.T. Elliff, (1947-1952). Houston attended his church until he graduated from high school in 1951.

Houston remembered Rev. Elliff vividly and talked about the promise he made to him, "not to smoke or drink until he was at least 21 years of age." Houston was 16 or 17 when he made that promise and he kept it to the very end.

Like Daniel, Houston "... *resolved not to defile himself with the royal food and wine, ...*" (Daniel 1:8 – NIV).

There were others, I'm sure, but these two men, in particular, greatly influenced Houston's life.

There were no churches for the deaf in Fordyce. However, a cousin, the late Dick Jones, pastor of Antioch Missionary Baptist Church in Little Rock in the 50s, would go to Fordyce and hold revivals for the deaf. He delivered his sermon in both voice and sign language. That was a great thing because many of the family members were saved during those revivals.

EARLY BASKETBALL THROUGH HIGH SCHOOL

Houston and his brothers loved to play basketball. A ball of any kind was hard to come by in those days. They did not have a basketball—instead they used an old tennis ball. The basketball goal was a coffee can with both ends cut out and nailed to the wall. That is how their love of basketball started. Basketball skills were honed and taken to their respective schools.

Fred and Clyde were both outstanding ball players at the Arkansas School for the Deaf. Fred played football and basketball, while Clyde devoted all of his time to basketball.

FRED NUTT - JUNE 10, 1922 - MARCH 15, 1983

Houston's oldest brother, Fred, was a member of the 1938 National Deaf Eleven Championship football team; 9-0-0. He also played on the 1940-1941 National Deaf Basketball Team that was undefeated with a record of 26-0.

Fred's oldest daughter, Patty, stayed connected to her "roots" by being a teacher at ASD for 30 years.

One day Fred came by the gym and Houston took him to the classroom and let him "peek in" where his daughter, Patty, was teaching her P. E. class. As Fred stood there watching silently, his eyes filled with tears. No doubt, he was overcome with a sense of pride—his daughter teaching deaf children at his alma mater. Houston and I shared this sentiment as well.

Houston and Patty are the only two from this deaf dynasty who chose to use their rich, cultural deaf inheritance to professionally work with the deaf. Others coming into this field may spend a lifetime and never have what they had.

CLYDE NUTT - JUNE 8, 1928 - MAY 2, 1979

1949 State Class B Basketball Champs: On March 12, 1949, the Arkansas School for the Deaf celebrated a 54-39 victory over Western Grove in the finals of the Class B State Tournament in Sheridan, Ark.

The win gave the Deaf School its first state title in the history of the school. Virtually the entire student body witnessed the exciting game between ASD and Western Grove. Clyde was an outstanding player and, in this game, he made 35 points—5 field goals and five free throws. Although he had outstanding performances all year, this could have been his best game.

Clyde was the second oldest brother and he graduated from Arkansas School for the Deaf in 1949. He made All-State in 1947, '48 and '49. In his senior year he averaged 25 points a game and he and his teammates shared the State B Basketball Championship Title. In 1948, he made the All-Southwest team and was selected on the All-District and All-State teams in 1949, which made it possible for him to play AAAD Basketball.

FAY NUTT – JULY 12, 1932 – JULY 14, 2012

Houston and his youngest brother, Fay, played for the Fordyce *Redbugs*. They were to play Helena in the opening game of the state tournament. Helena went ahead to win the game 44-38 and advanced to the quarterfinals. Fay and Houston scored all of the points except six but it was not enough to pull out a win. Fay made 18 points and Houston made 14.

Fordyce won two games and lost one in the semifinal. Houston was named to the first team All-State, thus beginning his recognition for excellence. There were eleven players selected by coaches for positions on the Class A All-State Honor Team and Houston was one of those players. (See Appendix 9.)

THE FORDYCE MASCOT

In the mid-1920s, the football team, along with the men from the community, cleared the land for a new football field. In doing this, they were eaten up with chiggers or redbugs.

> "Willard Clary suggested this tiny, annoying insect be used as the mascot and ever since they have been known as the Fordyce *Redbugs.*" - From the Dallas County Museum Calendar.

> "Fordyce boasts the only high school in America to claim the name *Redbugs* for its football team and, as one life-long resident adds, 'The only high school that would want to.'" - *The Last Coach* by Allen Barra, p. 6.

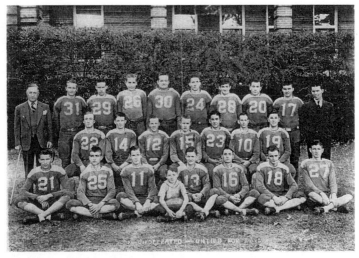

1938 Senior Football Undefeated and Untied: Top row: Supt. Henderson, Cleburne Harris, Glenn Robertson, Wayne Schieff, Alton Smith, William E. Fields, James Hicks, James Grimes, Robert Steed, Coach Van Cleve. Second row: Huffman, Vernon Voss, Bradford Gardner, Larren Musteen, Herman Woodward, Willie Brown, Audrey Fullbright. Bottom row: Augusta Howton, Euless Small, William Stewart, Water Boy Pat Henderson, Jerome Drake, Richard Leach, Fred Nutt, Bedford Rodman.

Front row: Howard Poe, Clyde Nutt, Jack Riley, Lawrence McCain, Maxwell Mercer, and Jodie Passmore. Back row: Howard Johnson, Billy Whitson, Charles Wilson, Victor Bulloch, and coach Edward Foltz.

Redbugs basketball team: Top row: Tommy Holt – manager, Ronnie Farrar, Earl Nutt, Will Green, Richard Mahan, coach Aramtis. Bottom row: Jimmy Raney, Fay Nutt, Herman Gray, Bobbie Fielder, and Houston Nutt.

NUTT BROTHERS SPELL HOOP
SUCCESS FOR FORDYCE TEAM

An article in *Arkansas Gazette*, January 2, 1950 read:

> "The greatest basketball players Fordyce has produced are three Nutt brothers, Clyde, Houston and Fay. They are the sons of Mr. and Mrs. Ab Nutt.
>
> "Houston Nutt is playing his third year as a *Redbug* and has the fans and coaches applauding his wizardry. Not only is he pouring the shots through the hoops, but his ball handling is uncanny.
>
> "Playing as a junior, he made first team All-State in 1947. With the senior team last year he averaged 23 points a game and reached a high of 42 points in one contest. He is 19, 6-2, and weighs 165 pounds.
>
> "Last year during an invitational tournament, the late Coach Bob Cowan said, "Houston is the best high school player I ever saw and could play on any college team in the state.
>
> "Against Magnolia he played less than three-quarters but tallied 28 points.
>
> "Coach Marvin Lindsey said, 'Next time I play against Houston Nutt I'll use a lasso. That's the only way to guard him.'
>
> "Houston is a junior and has another year with the *Redbugs*.
>
> "Fay Nutt is the younger brother and performed as a junior last year. He is 6-2, weighs 160 pounds and is 17. Playing with the juniors he averaged 17 points a game. In one tournament tussle he made 36 points.
>
> "He became eligible as a senior player this week and will add strength to the team at center.

"Clyde, a graduate of Arkansas School for the Deaf in 1949, was an outstanding player. He was 5'11" and weighed 162 lbs."

HOUSTON SR.

"Although Houston was good in football, it was as a high-scoring, six-foot-two-inch guard in basketball that he achieved 'all everything' status. Houston's basketball prowess was never equaled before or since," said Jack Gresham, superintendent of Fordyce High School.

It has been said by different people that Houston was an outstanding ball handler with skills ahead of his time. He scored 30-40 points in a game when the team score was seldom over 50. By the time he was a sophomore, he was getting recognition and filling gymnasiums in south Arkansas towns.

Houston in Redbugs uniform

Fay, Houston and Clyde, 1950

Basketball team: Back row: Scorekeeper Billy Don Lynn, Lavon Williams, James Oliver, George Turner, David Smith, and Coach William Martindale. Front Row: Don Hillman, Billy Helms, George Rogers, Houston Nutt and Buddy Fields.

QUARTERBACK AT FORDYCE HIGH SCHOOL

"Houston was a magician in hiding the football on hand-offs in the T-formation, a new offensive play at the time," said Jack Gresham, superintendent Fordyce High School.

In football, the big rivalry was the Camden Panthers where David Pryor was a star player. Whenever our paths cross, David never fails to mention the great times they had when his Camden Panthers met the Fordyce *Redbugs* in football rivalries.

Coincidentally, David Pryor and Houston had major heart attacks on the same day—Houston in Little Rock and David in Washington D.C. During their recovery, they visited not only about the heart attacks but their football rivalry. They jokingly blamed the Redbug Cafe in Fordyce and the Duck Inn Cafe in Camden for their heart attacks. Obviously, they had consumed many hamburgers in those places during those *Redbug* and Panther football-playing days.

Upon David Pryor's move to Washington, D.C. to become our U.S. Senator, his son, Mark, lived with us while he finished out the semester at Little Rock Central High School. He is the same age as our fourth son, Dennis. Today, Mark is our U.S. Senator and, it goes without saying, we are very proud of him.

The years David Pryor was governor of Arkansas coincided with our time at the Arkansas School for the Deaf and he helped the school in so many ways. Governor Parnell (1928 - 1933) was not the only governor of Arkansas to take a special interest in ASD.

David Pryor, Dennis and Houston at War
Memorial Stadium, November 23, 1986

Jim Bailey, sports editor of the *Arkansas Democrat Gazette* wrote the following in a letter dated 5-18-'08:

> "Mrs. Nutt,
> "As I mentioned in our telephone conversation some time ago, during Houston's high school days, he was by far the hottest basketball attraction in south Arkansas.

"I first saw Houston play during his junior year, 1949 -1950. His brother, Fay, was also on the Fordyce *Redbug* team at the time. Fordyce was in a conference with schools like Magnolia, Camden, Hope, etc., and when the *Redbugs* visited those schools, they generally played to sellout crowds thanks to Houston's gate appeal.

"Magnolia was and is the largest town (and the county seat) of Columbia County. People from the smaller communities in that county would go flocking into Magnolia for a Fordyce-Magnolia game. Not that they had any rooting interest in either team, they were there only to watch Houston play.

"I saw Houston play two or three times in high school, twice against Magnolia, and in a district tournament game between Fordyce and Emerson at Thornton, Arkansas. In February 1950, Don McMahen, an Emerson player, said he couldn't sleep all week after his coach told him he'd be guarding Houston Nutt in the district tournament.

"I kept track of Houston the best I could at Kentucky and Oklahoma State, but I never met him until after I started working for the *Arkansas Gazette* in 1956, the year you and Houston came to Little Rock to join the Deaf School staff.

"Quite simply, Houston was several basketball generations ahead of his competitive time. A tall guard, he amounted to what coaches called the 'The Total Package,' handling the ball, shooting from outside, driving for the basket, rebounding and, above all, doing everything with intensity, flair and enthusiasm. He often scored 30 to 40 points, and this was in a period of time when 40-50 was a fairly typical high school basketball score.

"Houston Sr., as a Fordyce basketball prodigy in the middle of the 20th century, is at least three to four decades ahead of his time.

"Sincerely, Jim Bailey"

LEGENDARY COACHES

Unbeknown to Houston one day he would play for two legendary coaches in his college career.

"Houston is undoubtedly the only basketball player to perform in college for both Rupp and Iba, the 'winningest' coaches college basketball has ever known," said Orville Henry, sports editor of the *Arkansas Gazette* and later the *Arkansas Democrat-Gazette*.

That phrase was written more times than any one could ever imagine over a 49-year period. Any time Houston Sr.'s name was mentioned, those two coaches' names were mentioned as well. It was indeed a distinguished honor and privilege for him to have played for Adolph Rupp and Hank Iba. (See Appendix10.)

ADOLPH RUPP - SEPTEMBER 2, 1901 - DECEMBER 10, 1977

The first legendary coach for whom Houston Sr. would play was Adolph Rupp, at the University of Kentucky, 1951-1953.

Coach Rupp accumulated 879 wins, from his arrival in Lexington in 1930 to his last game in 1972. He won 27 Southeastern conference titles and led the Kentucky Wildcats to four national championships. Winning was his passion.

I was reading a book about Dr. Vaught, and I came upon this story, which had a connection to Adolph Rupp! It's a *"small world."

"Worley Oscar Vaught, father of Dr. W. O. Vaught Jr., taught school in Versailles, Kentucky. Among the students he had in his classes were two boys who were later to become famous. One was

---

* small world - something we say when a person knows someone you know

a little fellow known as Happy Chandler, who would one day be governor of Kentucky. The other little boy was full of pep and loved games of all kinds. His name was Adolph Rupp, who later made national fame as the great basketball coach at the University of Kentucky. Worley Oscar, in later years, laughingly said that each one of those boys got a good licking every other day." - *Woven* by Marilyn G. Viala.

HENRY 'HANK' IBA - AUGUST 6, 1904 - JANUARY 15, 1993

The second legendary coach for whom Houston would play was Coach Henry "Hank" Iba, Oklahoma A&M, 1953-1956.

He held the dual position of basketball coach and athletic director until he retired in 1970. As OSU's athletic director, he built a program that won 19 national championships in five sports: basketball, wrestling, baseball, golf, and cross country. Coach Iba won 767 games during his coaching career, which was the second-most in college basketball history at the time of his retirement.

Coach Iba had an office in Gallagher-Iba Hall after his retirement, and Dickey had the privilege of visiting with him on a daily basis.

Dickey played basketball at Oklahoma State (1977–1981) and he had this story to tell:

> "Coach Iba came to watch my practice every day. He sat in the bleachers on the third row. After practice, while still sweaty, I would run up there and sit down beside him just to listen to anything he might have to say. Coach Iba had great stories to tell as well as words of wisdom. He would say, "Son, wherever you are, it's big time; if you're on the college level, it's big time; if you're at high school or junior high, it's big time. Don't ever think because you're at a higher level you're a better coach than one at a lower level.
>
> "No matter, what the conversation was, Coach Iba would always go back to stories about my dad and his

great athletic abilities. I will never forget him saying, 'Your dad was a black man in a white man's body,' referring to his athleticism. Coach Iba's stories and words of wisdom will forever be treasured."

What a rare and awesome privilege it was for Dickey and Houston Dale to have had the opportunity to know Coach Iba, a renowned coach, friend, and mentor. They were equally privileged to have played in Gallagher-Iba Hall, where their dad played, and Houston Sr. was very proud of that, as well.

The Gallagher-Iba Hall was known as Gallagher Hall for five decades before the name was amended to honor the former Oklahoma State basketball coach, Hank Iba, in 1987. During renovation, former players could have their jersey number and name put on the back of a seat for a fee. One of those seats has Houston Sr.'s name and number on it—thanks to his sons.

The Nutt family and Coach Iba's family have something in common. Coach Iba is the oldest of four brothers who are all basketball coaches and our four sons are basketball and football coaches.

Coach Iba died on January 15, 1993, in Stillwater, Okla.

Houston in Wildcat uniform

University of Kentucky Wildcats – 1951-52. Houston at bottom right

CHAPTER 4

HOUSTON'S COLLEGE DAYS

UNIVERSITY OF KENTUCKY

Houston chose to play only basketball in college, regardless of his athletic abilities. He grew up playing basketball with his brothers and was recognized for his basketball skills by several major colleges. After visiting different colleges, he accepted the scholarship from the University of Kentucky, which was rated tops in the nation at that time.

Filled with courage and determination, he left home all alone and hitchhiked the 611-mile trek to Lexington, Ky. The only person Houston would know there, other than the coaches who recruited him, would be the football coach, "Bear" Bryant. The only way to stay in touch with family was by writing letters to each other. He would soon live in a community with a population of 100,000 and the capital of the thoroughbred horse industry, located 80 miles east of Louisville and 85 miles south of Cincinnati. The home court would be Memorial Coliseum and it could hold 12,000 people. That was huge compared to the little "cracker box" gym at Fordyce High School.

The distance between Fordyce, Ark., and Lexington, Ky., didn't seem to deter Houston's decision in choosing this top basketball program in the nation. Who wouldn't want to play with the likes of Bill Spivey, seven foot All-American center; Frank Ramsey, outstanding All-American; and Cliff Hagan, who was potentially one of the greatest prospects ever to don a Kentucky uniform.

When Houston signed with Kentucky he had no idea Adolph Rupp would one day be the legendary coach that he became.

Any time we were traveling through Memphis, Houston would always say to the boys, "See that old Memphis bridge? I've hitchhiked across that bridge many times and, when coming home, I was always glad to get to that bridge, because it was easy to get a ride from Memphis to Little Rock."

THE OUTLOOK FOR 1951 - 52

Sports Publicity Editor at U. K., Ken Kuhn, wrote:

> "The traditional 'Rupp fast-break' offense again will be on the bill of fare along with a generous supply of controlled break patterns as 'The Man in the Brown Suit' fields his 22nd Kentucky cage aggregation.
>
> "Houston Nutt hails from Fordyce, Arkansas, the hometown of U. K. football coach Paul Bryant. Selected to Arkansas All-State team last season along with teammate Charlie Keller from Jonesboro...he tops six foot easily and looks good on rebounding under the basket...can be expected to see relief duty this season." (See Appendix 11.)

FRESHMEN TRY OUT FOR VARSITY

Upon arrival, the freshmen were actually trying out for varsity competition due to the military draft associated with the Korean War. Coach Rupp told the players, "Dribble from one end of the floor to the other, shoot a right-handed layup, dribble back and shoot a left-handed layup. If you hear my whistle, go out through the side door nearest you and keep going." That meant you were finished.

The boys were trimmed down with each trip down the court. Houston said he was very nervous when the coach pointed his finger at him and said, "If I could take one player to war with me, it would be Houston Nutt."

He really didn't quite understand what the coach had said at first, but as the upper classmen slapped him on the back and congratulated him, he knew it was OK. Houston made the traveling squad that finished the regular season at the top of the national polls, 29-3.

HOUSTON'S FIRST GAME AT KENTUCKY

Houston was sitting on the bench next to Coach Adolph Rupp. Picture in your mind—a freshman kid sitting next to Rupp, this strict disciplinarian, who was yelling and squirming around as he waved his arms with elbows bumping Houston in the ribs. He had to be a little nervous. Kentucky was up 25-1 and Houston couldn't understand why the coach was so upset. He asked the player next to him, "What's the Coach mad about?" He said, "He's mad because the other team scored a point."

Houston's first game as a Kentucky Wildcat—sitting on that bench next to Coach Rupp—I'm sure was very different from being a *Redbug* in the little cracker-box gym in Fordyce.

POINT-FIXING SCANDAL

At first, Coach Rupp said it was impossible—then remembering some of the one-point losses in the Allstate Sugar Bowl, maybe it was possible. In the NIT in New York, the first-round opponent was Loyola of Chicago. Alex Groza was doing a poor defensive job against the slow Loyola pivot man, Jack Kerris. On offense he was not the man that had led them through a great season. Kentucky lost 67-56. Two years later they got the answer—the players were shaving points. Alex Groza, Ralph Beard, and Dale Barnstable were the first to be charged.

The team was not permitted to play a game during the entire 1952-1953 season. It was the most severe fine that had ever been placed on a university.

"The scandal hurt Coach Rupp so badly," said Coach Harry Lancaster, quoting from his book, *Adolph Rupp As I Knew Him*, pp. 29, 32, and 33.

During Houston's second year, 1952-53, the NCAA placed the University of Kentucky on probation for point-shaving.

The freshmen players were farmed out to junior colleges close to their homes and later they were to return to Kentucky. As it turned out, no one from the freshman class returned to Kentucky after the "death penalty."

LITTLE ROCK JUNIOR COLLEGE

Houston enrolled at Little Rock Junior College, now University of Arkansas at Little Rock. While there, he hitchhiked from Fordyce to Little Rock and back, which was a breeze compared to Lexington, Kentucky. He would arrive at Uncle Floyd and Aunt Mary's door in Little Rock just in time for breakfast. Aunt Mary was so gracious and pampered him with wonderful breakfasts of bacon and fried eggs that were perfectly prepared, according to Houston.

The plan was that he would return to Kentucky, but during a tournament in Tyler, Texas, Coach Henry Iba saw Houston play and persuaded him to become an Oklahoma Cowboy at Oklahoma A&M. Coach Iba convinced him that Stillwater, Okla. was much closer to home than Lexington, Ky.

HOUSTON TRANSFERS

In 1953, Houston transferred to Oklahoma A&M, now Oklahoma State University. To play for one legendary coach in a lifetime is indeed a privilege, but now Houston would have the opportunity to play for a second legendary coach during his college career—Coach Hank Iba.

According to transfer rules, he was red-shirted his first year and this time was well spent getting acquainted with a totally different style of ball. On the first day of practice at Oklahoma A&M, Houston learned the difference in a hurry. They were given a basketball and told to dribble down the court, and Houston beat everyone. Coach

Iba said, "Hold it! Hold it! Houston, I know you've been playing for Kentucky but here at A&M we walk the ball down. Get used to it."

Houston not only got used to Coach Iba's philosophy but he really liked it. It proved to be very beneficial in his coaching career and was passed down for generations to follow. Coach Iba was a great man, father figure, teacher/coach and mentor. He was the best!

EDDIE SUTTON, FRIEND AND TEAMMATE

While at Oklahoma A&M, Houston had the opportunity to play on the same team with Eddie Sutton. One day Eddie would share Houston's home state and coach one of his sons, Houston Dale. A few years later he would play against another son, Dennis.

In 1974, Eddie Sutton became the Arkansas Razorbacks head basketball coach and took the program to new heights, including NCAA appearances and in 1978—The Final Four.

Our oldest son, Houston Dale, although on a football scholarship, played basketball for Coach Eddie Sutton as a walk-on (1976-1978), when they won the Governor's Cup in Brazil. Dennis, our fourth son, played for the late Coach Killingsworth at Texas Christian University which was in the Southwest Conference. This meant that Dennis and the TCU Horned Frogs would be playing against Eddie Sutton's Razorbacks.

Before the Razorback/TCU game, Eddie Sutton teasingly talked with Dennis about his making 36 points against Houston. Coach Sutton said, "We can give you 20 points, but not 30." In spite of Coach Sutton's admonition, Dennis made 32 points against the Razorbacks in that game. He said probably the most memorable time was winning the southwest tournament game against the Razorbacks, which was played during his sophomore year at the Reunion Arena in Dallas.

Years later in conversation, Joe Kleine, who played for the Razorbacks during that period of time, told us that he asked Coach Sutton, "Is Dennis Nutt from Arkansas? Why is he not on our team?"

Eddie Sutton did a good job for Arkansas from 1974 to 1985, even if he didn't recruit my son.

Houston in Oklahoma Aggies uniform

Houston in action

Houston (third from right), sitting on bench with players and coach Iba, watching clock during a close game in 1955.

Greenbrier - March 14, 1976

Houston (far right) with three U. of A. basketball coaches, Tom Skipper, Pat Foster and head coach Eddie Sutton as they watch the Conway Wampus Cats against the Monticello Billies in the state tournament

Oklahoma A&M (now OSU) library

Houston and Emogene as students.

HOUSTON MEETS FUTURE WIFE

While I was a student at Oklahoma A&M (now OSU), a tall, handsome guy came strolling through the library with a friend and just happened to sit down at my table. After a while, he got my attention and said, "Do you know me?" My reply was, "No, I don't know you."

In so many words, he explained he had played basketball for Adolph Rupp at Kentucky, transferred to Oklahoma and now was playing for Coach Iba. I was not impressed, since I knew absolutely nothing about basketball. Furthermore, I was not at all interested.

After this puzzling or at least unusual introduction, I would occasionally see Houston on campus. He kind of stood out, because he was at least a head taller than most everyone else and he had this huge smile and big friendly wave.

Jack Grisham, Houston's high school superintendent, said, "Houston's skill in athletics sets him apart, but his politeness and personal good conduct held him in good stead both on and off the court." I would have to agree with that.

As time went on, I learned that Houston was definitely in the minority. He did not drink or smoke, never used bad language and he was a Christian—of that I was impressed!

Regardless of the unorthodox manner in which we met, we may never know the reason Houston strolled through the library on that particular night unless it was, indeed, to meet the one with whom he would spend the rest of his life. Never in my wildest dream would I have ever imagined that one day I would be Houston's wife, his personal barber, and yes, even care for those "calloused, hitchhiking, basketball feet!" Just as a friendly reminder—*someone greater than I washed feet!*

> "*Then he poured water into a bowl and began to wash the followers' feet, drying them with the towel that was wrapped around him*" (John 13: 5, Devotional Bible, NCV by Max Lucado).

47

Nonetheless, Houston met his future wife and his helpmate for the rest of his life, and our 49 years together had its beginning with a stroll through the library.

Houston and Emogene's vows at The Church of the Nazarene - Rev. J. W. South officiated

During Houston's senior year at Oklahoma A&M, he finally persuaded me to go see one of his basketball games. He had such a passion for basketball and when it was mentioned, I always wondered if we were talking about the same thing. I could not understand his passion and excitement about a mere game of basketball.

When I attended my first game, I was sitting two or three rows behind the team bench and I could see the coach chewing out the players during time-out. I could not understand why the coach seemed so upset with his players. I had no idea that's what coaches do!

Houston would tell his friends that he played the worst game of his life. Coach Iba said, "Son, what's wrong with you?" His reply was, "Well, my girlfriend came to see me play." Iba said, "Oh that explains it."

After having seen a college basketball game, did I better understand the passion Houston had for the game? I absolutely did not! But that would come later.

MY LOVE FOR GAMES WAS LEARNED THROUGH MY SONS

Fast forward to the mid-60s when we were blessed with a house full of little boys! Houston made sure they had a ball in their hands at a very early age. It was football in the fall, basketball in the winter, baseball in the summer and all kinds of ball in between—like backyard, even rainy day, indoor nerf games.

The games went year-round with each overlapping the other. We celebrated the victories and consoled them when there was a loss.

There were literally hundreds of games for the boys, starting out with Little League baseball, Boys Club basketball, and Y.M.C.A football. In addition, we had the Nutt Pee Wee games that were played before the Nutt Brothers' benefit games every Saturday night. Then we moved on to junior high, high school, AAU games, college football and basketball games, summer league, and there were even pro games with the Dallas Mavericks. I thought the games might one day be over—instead the number only increased.

As the years went by, my sons became coaches. During one period of time, all four sons coached separate teams. Then there were years when Dennis worked for Dickey and Danny worked for Houston Dale.

Along came 13 grandchildren, and they all played some kind of game. The only way to survive was to *L-O-V-E* games.

Sitting on those benches year after year, enduring the sun, heat, rain, snow and ice, as well as indoor games, I learned to love games. But not to the extent that Houston did—no one could or ever will enjoy a game as much as Houston! He couldn't understand why I ever wanted to go anywhere other than to see a ballgame.

My daughter-in-law, Cathy, is sure I have broken the Guinness book of World Records for the number of games I have attended.

GRADUATION AND OPTIONS

After graduating from Oklahoma A&M, Houston was eager to start his life's work. There were three options—when most would be happy to have one.

First, he had the opportunity to be a grad assistant under Coach Iba, which he considered a great honor. Second, the pro basketball team in Tulsa, the Phillips 66 Oilers, had offered Houston $5,000 to play. In the '50s, that was a huge amount of money and a great temptation—especially for one who didn't have any money. Third, he could coach at the Arkansas School for the Deaf in Little Rock, Ark.

Houston said he got off by himself and asked God what he should do. He believed that God has a plan for everyone. He turned down the grad assistant offer under Hank Iba, the Phillips 66 Oilers offer with the money and accepted the job as coach at the Arkansas School for the Deaf in Little Rock. He believed this was God's plan for his life.

Dr. George W. Truett said, "To know the will of God is the greatest knowledge; to find the will of God is the greatest discovery; to do the will of God is the greatest achievement."

CHAPTER 5

INTRODUCTION TO FAMILY AND ASD

*Back row: Fred, Clyde, Houston, and Fay. Front
row: Ella Reace, May, Ab and Ludie Bell*

MEETING HOUSTON'S FAMILY

The plans were that I would travel to Fordyce to meet Houston's
family in August. We were to be married soon; however, a date
had not been set.

With bags packed and filled with excitement, I was on my way to Arkansas, but I had no idea what was about to happen in my life. Finally, I arrived in Little Rock a few hours later than planned because of problems with the bus. Houston was there to meet me and, at last, we were on our way to Fordyce. There were miles and miles of pine trees, something we didn't have in Oklahoma—but all of that pales in comparison to what I'm about to tell you.

Shortly before we arrived in Fordyce, Houston said something like, "The people down here may have a little hard time hearing." I didn't know exactly what he meant, but when you're in love, nothing else matters.

Finally, when we arrived at Houston's home, he opened the front door and turned on the overhead light. His family was sitting there in the dark, except for a table lamp. They probably had been napping during the wait, which is understandable.

Houston introduced me to his mother and father. As I shook hands, Houston said, "My parents are happy to meet you." I turned, looked at Houston, then back at the parents as he was talking to them in sign language and I thought, *Oh my goodness, they can't hear or speak!*" All kinds of thoughts were running through my mind, as you can imagine. I realized they were all looking at me and I tried to act as if nothing was out of the ordinary, but it was far from it!

The introductions continued—a brother, Fay, and his sister, Ella Reace, and there was a little "hearing" niece, Margie, who later became my best friend. I was so happy there was one who could talk and hear normally.

With all the hand movements, I was astounded, as I looked on in disbelief, with eyes staring and mouth wide open. Houston would talk to his parents in sign language, using an "audible" word every now and then, as I watched in A-MAZE-MENT! Houston's words, "a little hard time hearing" kept going through my mind. I thought, *"Low and Behold, the whole family is deaf!"*

The dominant language, or one could say the only language, was "sign language!" I was appalled at how those flying fingers and hands were actually conveying a message. It was unbelievable! If you didn't know sign language you were lost and, for sure, I was lost! As I was trying to take it all in, it was time to say good night—in sign language. Houston tried to teach me as he explained: "To sign 'good,' put your fingertips of the right hand to the lips; then it moves out and into a palm-up position on the upturned left palm. To sign 'night' the left hand with palm down is positioned at chest level. The downward right hand, a little above the left, moves over the left hand in an arc.

To him it was so simple!

The next day, one by one I met the other family members who lived nearby. It was more of the same and Houston would remind me to close my mouth from time to time. To put it mildly, I was overwhelmed with the discovery of deafness and sign language, not to mention deaf culture, in which I was totally immersed—although I didn't know it existed.

Deafness was not the only thing I experienced. I also discovered I was in the Deep South and people I met in Fordyce spoke with such a southern dialect or maybe even more of a "Cajun" accent. They used phrases like; "Y'all come back there here," which was barely comprehensible.

Fordyce was hot and humid! Not a bit of air seemed to stir and the leaves on the trees hung lifelessly. I never dreamed I would miss the "O-K-LA-HOMA WIND!"

I had been introduced to a new world like nothing I had ever seen before in my life. Although I left with more knowledge than with which I came, it was not nearly enough! But I made it through.

MY INTRODUCTION TO ARKANSAS SCHOOL FOR THE DEAF

On my way home to Oklahoma, Houston took me by the Arkansas School for the Deaf to show me where he would be working and there my plans took another turn. Tell God your plans and He will laugh!

> *"For, I know the plans I have for you,"* declares the Lord, *"plans to prosper you and not to harm you, plans to give you hope and a future"* (Jeremiah 29:11 – NIV).

Administration Bldg. on Deaf School campus

The administration building was the center of attraction and a grand, majestic three-story building.

At the front of the building there was a long flight of steps leading up to the entrance overlooking the city. The front door opened into a large, inviting room with high ceilings, large wingback chairs, and a rug covering the center of the wooden floor. The administration offices and guest rooms were off that big room. The superintendent's residence was on the second floor. The Home Economics classes were on the third floor and the cafeteria was on the ground floor.

There was a large, sprawling, covered breezeway leading to the dormitories on either side—the boys' dormitory extended on the right and the girls' dormitory on the left. The large covered area was a popular social-gathering place. It was always cool there with a soft breeze flowing through the breezeway. Besides it being the students' favorite place to gather with their friends, it was a multi-purpose area. At the beginning of the school year, tables were set up for registration. Remember there was no air conditioning in those days.

Yes, the Arkansas School for the Deaf was impressive! The campus was a beautiful place with the buildings nestled on a hillside on two tracts of land overlooking the Arkansas River on one side and Markham Street was at the bottom of the knoll on the other side— what a beautiful memory! (See Appendix 12.)

That building was torn down in 1962 and some had mixed feelings—including me. It was replaced with a new one-level administration building with dormitories and a house for the superintendent. These are the buildings you see there today.

SUPERINTENDENT AND MENTOR

There to greet us was Mr. Roy G. Parks, superintendent at ASD. He lived on campus with his wife, Fern, who taught there, and their third son, Kenny.

Mr. Parks coached his son in Little League baseball and Houston volunteered to help. That was the beginning of Houston's Little League volunteer coaching, which would span 30-plus years, along with his coaching career.

Mr. Parks immediately started talking to me about being a teacher for the deaf. The thoughts were swirling in my head! I had always wanted to be a teacher, but I had never in my wildest dream thought of being a teacher for the deaf. How could I? I couldn't sign and I couldn't spell. All the information was overwhelming! He would not take "NO" for an answer! He continued to tell me all the reasons I should be a teacher for the deaf and strongly encouraged me to enroll in the teacher preparation program at the school, which would begin September.

He was a great visionary and his plans were to get the Arkansas School for the Deaf accredited someday. This eventually became a reality. As the older teachers retired they were replaced with teachers who had college degrees.

At that time, there were very few teachers at the school who had a college degree. In earlier years the one-year program in teacher preparation was all that was required to teach any subject at any level. After completing the one-year program and three years of successful teaching, the teachers received teaching certificates.

Years later, when the school was accredited that certificate was no longer satisfactory. If you wanted to continue teaching at the school you had to take Deaf Education again—this time through a university.

In 1965 an off-campus center was established at ASD through the University of Arkansas, and I went through the Deaf-Ed program again. Miss Lucy Moore was our instructor. We completed the program in five summers by attending back-to-back sessions in the fifth summer.

I became a teacher for the deaf because of Mr. Parks' persistence and encouragement. He will always be remembered as a good man, a great educator of the deaf, a mentor and wonderful friend.

Mr. Roy G. Parks, Superintendent

Houston and Mr. Parks with Little League baseball team

EMPLOYEES LIVED ON CAMPUS

It was customary for houseparents, teachers and others to live on campus. Lorene and Race Drake lived in the girls' dorm with their two children, Freddie and Donna. They were deaf, as were their children. Mrs. Drake was a houseparent for many years. Mr. Drake, a graduate of Gallaudet College, was a printer at the *Arkansas Gazette* in downtown Little Rock. Although Mr. Drake was not employed at the school, the dorm was his home and his presence was an asset. On the days he didn't work he was a part of everything.

Edna and Arthur Crow lived in the dormitory as well. He was the Industrial Arts teacher in the Vocational Department at ASD for 52 years, and she was a houseparent for many years. They were deaf, as was their daughter, Alice.

In the early years, before the students were allowed to go off campus to church, Mr. Crow taught Sunday school in Parnell Hall on Sunday mornings.

Jeff and Leta Windham also lived on campus. He was the maintenance engineer and kept everything running smoothly. Mrs. Windham was a houseparent and Dean of Women for many years.

The students came home from school to a family atmosphere and someone was always there to discuss the good things about the day and help them through the bad times.

These families living on campus were great role models for the children.

The positive influence of these families was immeasurable and no doubt benefited the students throughout their lives. The three students who had deaf parents as teachers and houseparents at ASD went on to Gallaudet College and did very well, as did many of our other students.

LIFE IN THE DORM

Yes, Houston had whisked me off my feet and I landed at the Arkansas School for the Deaf in Little Rock, Arkansas. During our first year we lived on campus. Houston lived in the boys' dorm and I lived in the girls' dorm until we were married during the Christmas holidays.

The students felt more at home in the dormitories than with their biological parents, because so many parents could not communicate fluently with their children. The dorm was a treasured place where the deaf were the majority and hearing people were the minority or even outsiders. At first, I definitely felt like an outsider. It was also a place where they felt secure and their own sign language was the dominant language. Hearing people had to learn their language if they wanted to be accepted.

Life at ASD was as natural for Houston as breathing, because sign language was his first language and, as mentioned earlier, it was also his first school. He was one of them and he felt very much at home.

All of those dear people who worked there felt as if they knew Houston because of his brothers and other kin who went to school there years before. He was like family and was accepted the minute he stepped on campus. They even remembered his *"name sign."

A "name sign" was one more thing I had never heard of. The adult deaf thought my name sign should be the first letter of my last name, but the students overruled. They insisted that it be the same as Houston's, which was an "H" on the right side of the forehead, and my name sign is exactly the same, except with an "E," for Emogene.

Children like Houston, born to deaf parents, are given name signs at birth along with their names, while deaf children of hearing parents are given name signs when they come to school. Anyone associated with the deaf will have a name sign.

Unlike Houston, coming to ASD was a different story for me. Although it did help to have Houston there, I still had a long way to go. I knew nothing about their language much less their culture. I might as well have been on a foreign island. I had to write every word I wanted to say on a piece of paper and the deaf did the same for me.

---

* name sign - Ordinarily, children's name signs take the first letter of the first name and position it anywhere on the face, upper body or away from the body. However, adults coming into this field usually use first letter of last name.

All the houseparents and most of the teachers were deaf during the '50s. I had to learn a new language to understand and be understood, not to mention that I was totally immersed in deaf culture. I had a feeling that some of the older deaf were not totally in favor of sharing their language and residence with me. I had no idea what I had gotten myself into, and the hearing world that I knew had suddenly vanished. Now I was living in a world of deafness, and I felt completely lost in a wilderness of the unknown where words sometimes could "pierce the heart like an arrow!"

Tact doesn't seem to be a natural characteristic for the average deaf person. About the time I thought I was getting accustomed to the deaf, they would say something like, "Your hair looked better yesterday." If I should get a *"run in my hose," they would inevitably tap me on the shoulder and let me know about it.

When I first experienced this, I didn't know what to think. To say the least, it was unpleasant, and I thought it was very rude.

I discovered right away that I couldn't discuss my hurt feelings with Houston, because he was raised in a deaf environment and he thought as they did. I knew his response would be, "What's wrong with that?" That year living in the dorm I got a good **"taste of deaf culture!"

After surviving throughout the week, it was time for the real "Test." Our weekends were spent at Fordyce, the home of the *DEAF DYNASTY*—where the mother and father, the brothers and sisters, their families, the aunts, uncles, cousins and friends were deaf. It was overwhelming, to say the least.

The older deaf relatives and others who grew up at the deaf school in the early 1900s or before were straightforward and to the point! Wow! Needless to say, my skin was not nearly tough enough and, when you don't understand what is being signed, you automatically think they are talking about you. Yes, there were times that I would think, *"Oh Lord, what am I doing here?"*

---

* run in hose - a tear in hose
** taste of deaf culture - experiencing the deaf culture.

As time went by, I was learning to sign and spell under the students' tutelage and, with their trust and acceptance, those lonely feelings finally disappeared. Living in their midst, I had the opportunity to observe their facial expressions in all kinds of situations, and I became more familiar with all their deaf mannerisms and quirks. On a daily basis, I was learning volumes about their culture and language without being fully aware of it.

The things I learned from living in the dorm may have never been learned elsewhere, though it was difficult and even painful at times.

I attribute that experience as the foundation of sustaining my marriage to a husband of deep deaf culture. I am very grateful and appreciative for that experience.

LANGUAGE AND CULTURAL BARRIERS

My attention was drawn to an article in the *Arkansas Democrat-Gazette*, emphasizing the difficulty in learning a foreign language. The article was about a person doing everything he possibly could to learn the Japanese language and culture. He even took a trip to Japan but still it was tough. "The method recommended by experts," according to the article, "is to be born as a Japanese baby and raised by a Japanese family in Japan." I certainly understood what he was saying. Coming into the deaf world as a hearing person who is trying to learn the sign language and culture, I would say the same thing. The method I would recommend is to be born deaf to deaf parents and raised in a deaf environment, but if that is not possible, the next best thing is to live in the dormitory with deaf students.

Human beings are not the only ones who experience language and cultural barriers. Animals face the same difficulties.

In the spring of 2010, the offspring of the Panda bears that were loaned to the United States were returned to China. The Panda bears that were born in the United States were familiar with the English language only. When they arrived in China, there was a language problem, so their caregivers provided interpreters for the Pandas, making their transition a little easier. Whether people or Panda bears, it is a lonely place without a language!

MY INTRODUCTION TO TEACHING

Finally I was a teacher—but not the classroom teacher I had always envisioned. I was a language teacher in the high school department. My students couldn't hear or speak, and their language was foreign to me.

Being 23 years old, while some of my students were as old as 21, I was scared to death, as you can imagine. Concerning those big football players—the ones who always seem to slouch in their chairs—I wanted to say, "Sit up!" Yet, not being skilled in their language, it was hard to give commands.

It was not enough to know your subject matter; the biggest problem was communication. First and foremost, communication is paramount in knowing and understanding your students. Needless to say, I struggled my first year and used that teacher prayer more often than most, but I made it through.

AN EXPERIENCE THAT CHANGED MY TEACHING FOREVER

Early in my teaching career something happened that changed my teaching forever and I remember it as if it were yesterday. A little girl came to my class one day crying, uncontrollably. She was holding a letter in her hand, but I could not understand what she was saying because she was extremely upset. She finally showed me the letter and her mother had written, "I have worked so hard, I'm blue in the face,"—a phrase you and I take for granted. The little girl, of course, knew words like "face" and "blue." She also understood that blue was used in describing a bruise. She interpreted the phrase "blue in the face" as something being terribly wrong with her mother's face. You cannot imagine how difficult it was to convince the little girl that her mother was okay.

Sometimes our English language is difficult for hearing people, much less for people who can't hear it. Idioms and figurative speech that make up a large portion of our English language is especially difficult for the deaf. After deaf children have learned the literal meaning of a word—and it is used in a totally different way—it is absurd or, as in this case, most disturbing.

I decided from that day forward I would try my best to introduce an idiom and/or some kind of figurative language at every possible opportunity. That's exactly what I did in my language classes for those 30-plus years. In those early years there were no prepared materials on idioms, which is not the case today.

CHALLENGE FOR TEACHERS AS WELL AS STUDENTS

An idiom is a phrase whose meaning cannot be determined by the literal definition of the phrase itself and it must be taught to deaf students.

As mentioned before, idioms and figurative speech are found in just about everything we read—our newspapers, letters, books, and metaphors are used throughout the Bible—for example: Matthew 5:13-14 - NKJV *"You are the salt ... You are the light ... "* and John 10:9 - NKJV, *"I am the door ... "*

We also use idioms in our everyday conversation.

A friend of mine wrote a note to her niece who is deaf, telling her to go to the grocery store and buy *"stuff" for meat loaf. Needless to say, her niece came home **"empty-handed"—she didn't know what "stuff" was. The deaf can't just pick up the meaning of an idiom like the hearing child; it must be taught and we can't take for granted that they know it.

MY FIRST ATTEMPT TO TEACH AN IDIOM

As I sat at my desk, looking at all those papers waiting to be checked, I realized my desk was totally *"snowed under" with stacks of homework

---

* stuff – ingredients for meatloaf
** empty-handed – with nothing

papers from all six classes—a basketful of stories to be edited for our school paper, books, pencils, chalk, and numerous other things. I thought "snowed under" would be the perfect idiom to begin with and the cluttered desk would be the perfect visual aid to make reference to as often as needed. While speaking of cluttered desks, the late Ms. Lucy Moore who was the Deaf Ed Instructor at ASD said not once, but many times, "Teachers who have a neat desk are not good teachers!" Since my desk always seemed to be "snowed under," I loved that!

My first idiom lesson went something like this:

After gathering pictures that captured this concept of "snowed under," I taped them all over the boards and explained each picture over and over. Remember, for every step taken with the hearing, at least a half dozen or more steps are taken with the deaf. I then focused on my cluttered desk time and time again, pointing to all the things piled on it, making it a perfect example of "snowed under." I was so excited about teaching this idiom and felt good about the presentation with all the pictures—and my messy desk.

At last, when I felt SURE they all understood the new idiom, I handed a sheet of paper to each one and instructed them to draw a picture that would capture the concept of the idiom, *"snowed under." Again, I felt so good about the presentation and had no doubt everyone understood. When the students finished their papers, I collected the pictures and started flipping through them. I soon found out that all that explanation with pictures, even with my messy desk, had gone right **"over their heads." Just about everyone in the class had drawn pictures of people covered with snow, cars covered with snow, houses covered with snow, on and on. All of those good feelings had turned to disappointment!

I lost count how many times that lesson was repeated, but one day the students were able to draw the correct picture and write the correct meaning in their own expressive language. When that happens, you will want to shout, cry and you will want to teach to—E-TER-NI-TY!!! That is indeed a teacher's reward!

---

* snowed under- more work than can be done conveniently
** over their heads- did not understand

Emogene teaching at ASD

The Senior class of 1964-65 dedicated the Yearbook to Mrs. Nutt
"a teacher with a quiet smile and an understanding heart."

CHAPTER 6

HOUSTON BEGINS COACHING AT ASD

Perhaps Hebrews 12:1 says it best, *"Let us run the race that is before us and never give up"* (The Devotional Bible, NCV by Max Lucado).

It was September 1956 at the Arkansas School for the Deaf, 2400 Markham Street, Little Rock, Arkansas. Houston, in his native state and in a familiar place, was beginning his life's work or some would say—his mission in life. His beginning salary was $1,900 a year. He said many times if he had it to do over he would do the same thing.

Being a coach at the Arkansas School for the Deaf in the '50s meant not only a coach for basketball but for football, track, baseball or any other kind of coach needed. It also meant being a teacher and much more. Houston had great expectations for the work he wanted to accomplish. He not only wanted to coach basketball, he wanted to instill in the minds of his players and deaf kids in general that "by working hard you can achieve your goals, and do anything you want to do." He was the perfect one to instill that message because, simply by working hard, he earned a free education and landed his dream job. From his circumstances, what were the chances of this happening?

While I was, *"getting my feet wet" in my new world of deafness, Houston was in his element, standing on the brink of fulfilling his childhood dream. The thing for which he had waited his whole life,

---

* getting my feet wet - learning

he had before him: a group of boys, a basketball and a gymnasium. All that was missing was a coach!

I can see him now with all that energy there on the basketball court—his hands in the air giving instructions in his very own sign language, dressed in a white T-shirt and gray coaching shorts, white knee-high socks, white tennis shoes and a whistle around his neck.

TRAITS THAT MADE HOUSTON A GOOD COACH

Houston was young and full of energy and highly driven. His enthusiasm was contagious! His ability to arouse enthusiasm in others was a great asset. Ralph Waldo Emerson once said, "Nothing great was ever achieved without enthusiasm."

Houston was dedicated. He worked energetically and unrelentingly with hundreds and hundreds of boys throughout the years, not only the deaf but hearing as well. He was scrupulous in every aspect. He made sure that every player knew the fundamentals. He would conscientiously go over and over little things like holding the ball correctly at the free throw line and making sure the toes were lined up. Every task was repeated until it was done correctly. The hours he put in were unimaginable! He never seemed to physically tire nor did he ever tire of practices or games. It was as if he couldn't wait until the next one.

Motivation is a gift that all coaches don't have but all *great* coaches do. Houston could get his players so ready for a game. No doubt that helped him win many games because, for the most part, they played against better, stronger hearing teams and hearing teams had the advantage over the deaf.

"No one could inspire groups better at pep rallies. He communicated with kids so well. "He would have done well in drama," said Susan Pack, superintendent at ASD.

Houston was a strict disciplinarian. The kids described him with one word—*strict*—and they were very careful to do the right thing. He was very skilled in sign language (ASL) because of his deaf heritage and the kids naturally looked up to him. Whatever he said, they did without question and that brings the following incident to mind: One of my students was very meticulously explaining to a new student the things he should know. Unaware that I was watching, he said, "First, you have to be very careful in this class and not break any rules, because her husband is the coach, and the coach is very strict!" The word "strict" was signed very forcefully and was exaggerated. Then he spelled the word, Wow, and dangled his hand, shaking it up and down with raised eyebrows and furrowed forehead. I was so caught up by this dramatic explanation, I realized for a moment that my eyebrows were raised and my forehead was furrowed as well.

As time went by, the new student never misbehaved. I thought, *"Hmmm! I guess it doesn't hurt to have a good coach in one's corner"*— or maybe the credit goes to the one with that dramatic explanation!

Along with the traits mentioned above, enthusiasm, hard work and dedication, anything is possible! Houston had all the traits of a great coach, but in the world of deafness, there's one more— communication. He had that, too. He had a very colorful, illustrious way of communicating using ASL and, when he talked to the kids, you could hear a pin drop.

At the pep rallies, he would talk briefly and, while the cheerleaders found their places on the stage, Houston would point to the ceiling and say, "Do you see that light fixture up there? I want you, along with everyone in this auditorium, to make so much noise that it will shatter that fixture into a million pieces!"

Please know when Houston delivered a message he was not standing quietly in one position. He was moving all around the stage using so much energy and signing so forcefully! As one explained it, "The knuckles on the back of his hands would turn white!" If it were possible for the light fixture to be broken, it would have already been shattered before the kids got their chance.

HOUSTON HAD THE ABILITY TO BUILD GOOD TEAMS

Keep in mind that large numbers of great athletes were not flocking to the Arkansas School for the Deaf, but Houston produced an unbelievable number of good teams. A very small percent of the population in Arkansas is deaf and a smaller percent of the deaf school population will be good athletes.

Even though the numbers were very sparse, Houston managed, year after year, to have at least one good player and always seemed to produce a good team. He started with the nine- and ten-year-old boys so they would be ready by the seventh grade. Remember, for every step taken with the hearing, a half dozen or more steps are taken with the deaf. After much, much repetition and hard work, he somehow turned out good players every year and games were won in spite of the small percentage of great athletes. (See Appendix 13.)

THE MOST-ASKED QUESTION

Houston played for two legendary coaches, Adolph Rupp and Hank Iba; however, the style of basketball was as different as night and day. Houston was often asked, "Which style do you use in coaching the deaf?" He believed that every coach contributed, just as one's upbringing helps make you the person you are. Houston incorporated strategies and techniques from Rupp, Iba, and even his high school coaches, formulating his own coaching style that would work for the deaf. Largely, it depended on his players. I have heard him say so many times, "When I have speed I draw from Rupp's style, and when I don't have speed, I lean more toward Coach Iba's philosophy."

Houston used more of Coach Iba's methodical style in coaching the deaf, because he actually made mediocre players into good players—unless, of course, a phenomenal player came along.

Only once in a lifetime, if at all, will a coach have the opportunity to coach a phenomenal player, and Houston was one of those coaches who had the good fortune of experiencing this phenomenon!

DEAN OF STUDENTS: ONE OF MANY TITLES

Whichever title at whatever time, Houston seemed ready for each role. He would be at the school at 7 a.m. or before to solve any problem that might have occurred during the evening hours. The kids would be lined up to see him; however, most of the time there really wasn't a problem—it seemed they just wanted to see Houston. He would listen briefly, give them a big smile, a pat on the back and they were off to class. If there was a problem, he was the one to solve it in the shortest amount of time.

Somehow he always seemed to know exactly what the kids were up to; in fact, they referred to him as the FBI. I found that amusing, because when our sons were growing up they thought the same thing. Sometimes I thought he was a mind reader or he had a sixth sense, until I learned that every move I made was reported to Houston. Whatever happened in my classroom or elsewhere, the kids made sure he knew all the details.

Houston held the deaf kids and the school close to his heart at all times. Even during the times he was with family or just having a hamburger with his son, he was still very much at work. Dennis, our youngest, relates this story:

> "My dad and I were at McDonalds one day and a deaf man came in and handed the man behind the counter a card that said, 'I'm a deaf-mute, would you please help me?' My dad walked up to the young man, and asked what he was doing. Houston was the last person on earth that man wanted to see. He was told, in no uncertain words, to get out and never do that again or he'd be in jail! He couldn't get out of there fast enough! Hopefully, he never returned to that place or any other place asking for money. My dad was really upset with him and said there was no excuse for that."

Having grown up with deaf parents, Houston didn't have much patience for those who used deafness as an excuse.

In the 21st century, the deaf can pursue any profession and—thank the Lord—they are not perceived as they once were.

HOUSTON WAS ALSO A CLASSROOM TEACHER

Before Houston would coach any kind of ball, he would start his day teaching in the classroom, and after school he would teach physical education. At that time, P. E. was not part of the curriculum but rather was an after-school activity. That was all just fine with Houston. He never complained about long hours. He was so happy to be working with the deaf and being back in his home state. It couldn't get any better than that!

I hope you have been able to sense how happy Houston was to be at ASD. Fortunately, the students were equally elated to have him, according to one student's letter that was read at our retirement party. Among other things, she wrote:

> "I remember very clearly, as a first-year student in middle school at ASD, the arrival of handsome Houston and beautiful Emogene. Their arrival for us was like the arrival of Jackie and J. F. Kennedy in Washington, D. C. They were our Camelot.
>
> "Houston was our math teacher, but he taught us more about basketball than math. They were bright, fresh, and young. I love you both, Donna." (Donna Drake, a student at ASD, was a teacher/principal at Florida School for the Deaf in St. Augustine, Florida and is now retired.)

Houston worked not only from sunup to sundown but into the night and on weekends. My dad would say, "Houston, if you worked half as hard at any other thing, as you do with ball, you'd be a MILLIONAIRE!"

The long hours and hard work seemed to be Houston's delight, his joy and his whole life. And yes, he is a "millionaire" from blessings in sharing his rich cultural inheritance.

He went about his work vigorously, encouraging every boy he bumped into, to try out for basketball and he made it fun. Those who came out usually stuck with it until they graduated. If there were students with a physical handicap, he signed them up, too. Houston would make them managers or anything to be a part of the team. He made them feel like sweeping the floor was special. More often than not, many of their problems disappeared.

Houston had such a compulsion that every boy should play ball if at all possible. He knew from his own life that there were multiple benefits: to gain confidence; something to take pride in; to be disciplined and stay out of trouble; improve grades; or, to even experience their dream as he did.

Houston as a classroom teacher.

Houston's first class at ASD: Houston Sr., Donna Drake, Bette Hicks, Patty Person, Franklin Huckaba, Phyllis Robertson, Mary Lou Wilson, Wallace Tedder and Fern Pickett

Houston's ASD basketball team

HOUSTON COULD COMMUNICATE AT ALL LEVELS

Houston's ability to communicate, using sign language (ASL) at all levels, made him invaluable and he was a special blessing to the deaf students who were severely limited in vocabulary with little or no language.

In 1971, The Convention of American Instructors for the Deaf was held on our campus. Tents were set up and teachers at ASD were to make sure everything was running smoothly. As I passed by one tent, the speaker was talking about communication. I heard him say, "People here at ASD are so fortunate to have a person on campus who can communicate at all levels." I hesitated, as I was curious to see who that person was. He continued to explain the different levels: "Some have only words and gestures, some use ASL altogether. Others may have a good understanding of the English language and some may depend largely on finger spelling"—on and on. My mind was racing ahead, thinking of different people on our campus.

When he said, "That person is Houston Nutt," I should not have been surprised, considering Houston's background. He could definitely communicate at all levels. It was amazing to watch him talk with deaf students, those who were rooted deeply in deaf culture, as well as others. He would truly "light up their world." A flick of the hand, a gesture—it was unbelievable! He thoroughly understood them and vice versa. People who are not native signers can learn and do a good job but we will never have what they have.

It is a real blessing when one who has deafness in the family dedicates his or her life to work with the deaf. I don't know about all who fall into this category, but I do know Houston Sr. could motivate the deaf to their fullest potential. Yes indeed, the students at ASD were fortunate to have had Houston Nutt, Sr. on campus.

Elaine Scott, Arkansas State Board of Education (1985-1997) said, "Houston contributed so much to the school and to the state. His example made generations of students better people. I admired greatly his caring and long service to those students."

Coach Ed Teeter, (retired) of San Marcos, Texas, said, "His influence will be felt in the state of Arkansas for generations of students."

JOB PLACEMENT/INTERVIEW

Houston had many roles at the school: teaching, coaching, athletic director, dean of students and some of his roles did not have titles. He placed many students and former students on various jobs. He didn't just place them but checked on them constantly and routinely went to the places of business to resolve a communication breakdown. He not only worked with the kids during the school year but all through the summer months as well.

Our dear friend, the late R.V. Strickland, managed the Golden Host Cafeteria in Little Rock during the 70s and 80s and he so graciously employed many of our students during those years.

On one occasion, Houston had made arrangements for a former student to be interviewed for a job. He went to the interview, nicely groomed and prepared to put his *"best foot forward." A short time later, he was back in Houston's office with a puzzled look on his face. When Houston asked him what had happened, the young man

---

* best foot forward - do your best

handed Houston the paper on which they had corresponded. The young man had written: "I want your job." The employer replied, "That job is filled." The interview was over.

The English language was and is a huge problem for students and the troublesome pronouns definitely don't help. With a phone call, Houston explained the young man really didn't want his job; rather, he wanted a job if there was one available. Everything was *"squared away," as well as a huge chuckle with the man who filled that job! The young man was placed on a job at the Finkbeiner Meat Packing Company and stayed there over 20 years.

Today, there is job-placement program for the deaf and people are now paid a salary for the job Houston did for free during those earlier years.

A STORY HOUSTON LOVED TO TELL

Early in Houston's career at ASD, he received a call from the coach at the Arkansas School for the Blind challenging him to a softball game. The coach must be joking—softball, blind school? The coach called back to say they wanted to play at night. Now Houston was confused! He thought the coach surely must be teasing. So, Houston called him back and said, "Now let me get this straight. You want your blind boys to play a softball game with my deaf boys at night?" The coach answered, "Yes, our boys can see better under the lights."

Houston got his deaf boys together and explained the game plan. In spite of his admonition not to take this game lightly, the boys thought it would be no contest. To make a long story short, the blind school team beat the deaf school team. The deaf boys were "bummed out." They couldn't believe it. They were a little embarrassed and some were even angry and they begged to play them one more time. That did not happen, and I know some are still angry today. Maybe they learned a good lesson: Never go into a game thinking you are better than the other team; therefore, lacking your best effort.

---

* squared away - properly taken care of

TELL IT TO THE JUDGE!

Bill Wilson sent us a copy of this letter he wrote to the superintendent at ASD:

"Dear Susan,

"I thoroughly enjoyed the article in the Gazette on March 30, 1988, about Mr. and Mrs. Nutt and their family. There is one talent of Coach Nutt, however, that was not mentioned.

"Several years ago I was sitting in as special judge for Jack Holt, Sr. A couple of young lads from the school had attempted to rob a liquor store with a water gun. Since attempted robbery is a serious offense, it was almost certain that they would be 'bound over' to Circuit Court for jury trial on felony charges, (even though the attempt would have been laughable had it not been such a serious matter—they turned and ran almost as soon as they walked into the store.)

"They showed up with Coach Nutt as their counsel. He pleaded with me not to send them over to Circuit Court since they were basically real good boys from good families. (He had the mamas and papas in the courtroom for me to see, too.) Of course, I did not have the authority to reduce a felony to a misdemeanor so they could be handled in Municipal Court, but after he stayed after me, I passed the case until a later date when I would sit as Judge again. The same thing happened two or three times in succession.

"Finally, the deputy prosecutor talked with the liquor-store owner and they agreed to reduce the charges to a misdemeanor. This was done and the boys were put on a first-offenders program. I kept up with them for a year or two and they did fine. As good a coach as Houston was/is, I have always wondered if he didn't miss his calling. In any event, I am very pleased to see that the school has honored them, because the Nutts are high-type individuals in all respects.

"Cordially, Bill Wilson"

Houston took responsibility for the boys by putting them to work every day for the rest of the summer. For the most part, they worked at our house and I prepared their meals. It was all worth the time and effort. When school started, they lived in the dormitory under close supervision and they did great. Years later, one of the young men showed up on our front porch with his family to say "thank you" for what Houston had done for him. For coaches, nothing is more important than winning games or a championship—unless, of course, it would be a player coming back to say —*"Thank you!"*

SCOREBOARD

When we came to the Arkansas School for the Deaf in 1956, we didn't have a scoreboard on the football field. The score was kept by someone standing on a platform, manually changing the numbers as the score changed. You can imagine how excited Houston was to get a new electric scoreboard.

Dear friends like Bill Luplow, the late Bob J. Linebarier and Jerry Davis of Affiliated Foods made this happen. How Houston appreciated this act of kindness as well as their lasting friendship!

*Houston shakes hands with Bill Luplow (far right), president
of the Razorback Letterman's Club, and Bob J. Linebarier, past
president, at the ceremony dedicating the new electric scoreboard.
The Razorback Letterman's Club and Affiliated Food Stores, Inc.
were responsible for buying the scoreboard in the early 70s.*

HOUSTON'S HOBBIES

Mr. Roy G. Parks, superintendent at ASD, had German shepherd
dogs, and he recruited Houston to help with the obedience training.
As they worked together, Houston took an interest in dogs and in
their training. Houston bought a German shepherd puppy and when
his dog was old enough he started obedience training with him as
well. They took the dogs to all kinds of meets in the state as well
as out-of-state and from those meets silver bowls, silver-trimmed
coasters and silver trays fill the bookshelves.

SAM BO WINS 1ST PLACE

In the spring of 1973, Houston took his German shepherd, Sam Bo,
to Oklahoma City. He didn't travel across country with an elaborate
motor home, kennel or groomer like many of the dog owners. He
drove Sam Bo all the way from Little Rock to Oklahoma City on the
floorboard of his car and won 1st place. He brought home the first

place ribbon, certificate, and a silver bowl engraved with these words: "Highest Scoring Dog in Trial."

More German shepherds followed Sam Bo before Houston switched to Doberman Pinchers in the mid-seventies. He loved to show-off his dogs, especially when company came. The dogs would sit, stay, lie down, play dead, get on the rock and stay there until commanded to do otherwise. He continued to train our dogs, but he never showed the dogs in meets after winning first place at the Oklahoma City meet.

For the longest time after Houston's death, Pleasure, his Doberman Pincher, was very despondent and refused to eat. I was told to give the dog something that belonged to Houston, so I gave him a pair of Houston's pants and he would drag them everywhere he went for the longest time.

After all other efforts were exhausted, my neighbors, Kenny and Janis Scott, made friends with Pleasure and Keegan, riding them in their golf cart almost on a daily basis. Kenny worked them out and let them perform for him. All were happy.

OLD CARS: A RIDE FOR A FUTURE PRESIDENT

Houston loved to buy old cars and fix them up. One day I needed to go to the grocery store so Houston said he'd take me in his "new," old car. I was not very happy about that, because I knew there was a hole in the back floorboard.

We were driving down Markham Street and we saw Governor Bill Clinton standing on the side of the street. That was during the interim between his two terms as Governor. There was no traffic and Houston made a U-turn in the middle of Markham Street and asked Mr. Clinton if he needed a ride. Looking a little surprised, he said, "Yeah." He opened the back door and got in. I thought, *"Oh no! He could stick his foot through that hole."*

He and Houston talked all the way to his home in the Heights, as I held my breath. We made it safely without a mention of the hole and without him sticking his foot through it. Our best regards were given for baby Chelsea as we said, "good-bye." It was no surprise to us that Bill Clinton seemed just as relaxed in that "new" old car with a hole in the floorboard as he would later feel in his presidential limousine.

OFFICIATING

When Houston was not coaching some kind of ball, he was officiating. On some Saturdays, he would umpire all day long for $3 a game. He umpired adult male and female games but when he was umpiring the little boys' baseball games and/or the little girls' softball games, he was in his element. Parents would tell me their children would be so excited when Houston called their games. The reasons were basically the same. They said he always talked to them and gave them words of encouragement. Chances are he told them, "You're the best!"

He also trained many of the officials who are officiating in Arkansas today. He would give them a whistle and tell them to come to ASD and referee the "B" games in basketball or junior varsity football.

Houston and Howard Hughes officiating

Houston with Sam Bo

Granddaughter, Hanna,
with Patience

Houston with Bubba

Emogene with Keegan

CHAPTER 7

PLAYER/COACH

MILAN, ITALY

During those early years of coaching at ASD, Houston, along with his brother, Fay, joined the AAAD (American Athletic Association for the Deaf) to play basketball with their older brother, Clyde. The team traveled to Dallas, Houston—all over the southwest to play ball.

The three Nutt brothers largely made up this team known as the Little Rock Silents. To qualify for the World Olympics, they first had to defeat Milwaukee in the national championship game in New York's Madison Square Garden. The game went into overtime. Fay made 12 points to win the national crown and plans were being made for Milan.

Money was raised for travel through benefit games. The late Bennie Craig, (Channel 11), whose signature phrase was, "It doesn't cost a penny to be a good sport," was instrumental in promoting them. The generous donations from over the state of Arkansas made it possible for them to get to New York's Madison Square Garden.

About the time they were to leave to go to Milan, their father, Ab Nutt, passed away. They were delayed because of his death and funeral service. Albert "Ab" Nutt died from a massive stroke on August 8, 1957. He had been partially paralyzed for eight years from a previous stroke at age 52.

After the funeral service was completed and everything taken care of, Houston and his brothers caught up with their teammates in Amsterdam. From Amsterdam the team visited Belgium, Germany and Austria before arriving in Milan for the meet.

In addition to the United States, nations that competed were: Argentina, Austria, Australia, Belgium, Bulgaria, Czechoslovakia, China, Denmark, Finland, France, Germany, Great Britain, Hungary, India, Iran, Israel, Italy, Yugoslavia, Norway, New Zealand, Holland, Poland, Romania, Spain, Switzerland, Sweden and Uruguay.

The Nutt brothers, Clyde, Houston, Fay, along with J. L. Jackson and Jody Passmore were the "Unbeatable Five," according to the AAAD Bulletin. In the opening game the Silents defeated Finland 57-30, walloped France 51-21, romped to an 89-39 victory over Italy, and soundly defeated Belgium 81-25 for top honors in the world tournament.

In addition to winning the title of 1957 World Basketball Champions, they had the privilege of touring six European countries and visited 10 major cities. They also enjoyed the Rome Festival, Riviera Lake, Lucerne and Paris.

The United States, under the jurisdiction of the AAAD, was represented by 40 athletes who included the 1957 national basketball champion team, Little Rock Association of the Deaf, and were led by an official delegation of officers and coaches: Messrs. Robey Burns, Al Fleischman, Art Kruger, Tom Elliott, Charles Whisman, Tom Berg, Ray Butler, Lonnie Tubb, L.C. Shibley, and Joseph Worzel. Rooting for the Stars and Stripes banner bearers were some 200 other American fans.

AN UNFORGETTABLE WELCOME HOME!

When they returned home, the *"red carpet" was rolled out for the Silents. An official delegation from the Little Rock Chamber of Commerce was on hand to greet the team. Chamber president

---

* red carpet – ceremonial welcome

William Shepherd said, "They have brought more honor to us than themselves and at a time when honor is thin." Alderman Franklin Loy presented each of the players a Key to the City of Little Rock. Secretary of State C. G. "Crip" Hall presented the players with official Arkansas Traveler Certificates and remarked at length about the great publicity the team had brought to Little Rock.

A police escort led them down Main Street and out to the Arkansas School for the Deaf, where their families and friends were gathered to congratulate them on winning the World Championship Game in Milan, Italy, and for bringing home the Gold!

Silents basketball team—AAAD world champions in Milan, Italy:
Front row: Wesley Hardgraves and Jody Passmore (holding ball);
Back row: Luther Shibley, Clyde Nutt, Fay Nutt, J. L. Jackson,
Maxwell Mercer, Bill Hopkins, Houston Nutt and Lonnie Tubb

Fay and Houston "holding up" Leaning Tower of Pisa

Clyde, Fay and Houston with two unidentified people in Milan, Italy

Luther Shibley and Houston study plans for competition

CLYDE'S AAAD BASKETBALL EXPERIENCE

Clyde made the All-Southwest team in 1948 and in 1949 was selected for the All-District and All-State teams, making him a contender in the AAAD. He played his first AAAD tournament in Washington, D. C., following his senior year. The rest is history, as the saying goes. It was the start of a long and productive career in the AAAD tournaments that produced five records.

Clyde played 14 years in AAAD nationals on teams that produced 28 wins and 14 losses. He was named Most Valuable Player twice in the tournaments in 1951 and 1953. For eight years, Clyde played in the national finals and three years in the national championship games.

He was the only player in the history of the AAAD to score more than 1,000 points in the national meets—1,015 in 42 games. He reached the 1,000-point plateau in the national meet at Boston in 1966 at the age of 37. The game was stopped and he was presented the game ball before a standing ovation. No one else has accomplished this record in that league.

Clyde was selected AAAD Athlete of the Year in 1966. The three brothers were instrumental in getting the Silents to the World Olympics in Milan, Italy, in 1957, winning the world Championship.

All three brothers were inducted into the American Athletic Association of the Deaf Hall of Fame for basketball: Clyde in 1975 in Bridgeport, Conn.; Houston in 1986 in Baltimore, Md.; and Fay in 1992 in Little Rock.

When the Little Rock Silents returned home from winning the world-championship tournament in 1957, Jim Bailey, sports editor for the *Arkansas Democrat-Gazette* said:

> "I was assigned to meet the plane and do interviews at the old Adams Field airport. There I had my first conversation with Houston.
>
> "Over the years we became very good friends, especially during the summer of 1975, when I haunted the Nutt household for weeks putting together the

story on Houston Dale and the Nutt family's athletic history."

AAAD GAMES CONTINUE

After winning the national tournament in New York and the World Championship in Milan, Italy, the Nutt brothers continued to play a few more years for the AAAD Association.

During a game in Chicago, Houston fell and did a back flip to get up, which can be very damaging. In Houston's case, three discs were ruptured. After bed rest, he would try to play again only to make it worse. Eventually he had to have back surgery. They continued to play but it was beginning to be a burden on the families, especially the out-of-town and out-of-state games.

Juggling AAAD basketball, work and family was our way of life for more than a decade. Our four sons were born during those AAAD basketball years: Houston Dale in 1957, Dickey in 1959, Danny in 1961, and Dennis in 1963. Houston was never at home because he was always playing ball. To put it mildly, it was a challenging time. Finally, he and his brothers decided it was time to give up AAAD basketball and play closer to home. That was a day of rejoicing!

A NEW ERA: PLAYING FOR CHARITY

Instead of playing for championships, the brothers played for charity, giving back to their home state. It was a family affair, including the dads, moms and all the children. Everyone enjoyed the games and life-long friendships were acquired.

Houston was the coach, a player and the coordinator, scheduling games from one end of the state to the other—from Walnut Ridge to Prescott, Newport to Fordyce and even "a place called Hope." Every Saturday night there was a game for charity—Heart, Cancer, United Fund, athletic programs or for anything else needed in the community.

One special Saturday night, the little Fordyce gym was packed for the United Fund Charity. Extra players were picked up for each game and, from time to time, the extra player would be a high-profile athlete. On this occasion, it was Lance Alworth who was an All-American halfback at the University of Arkansas in 1961. He later played for the San Diego Chargers of the American Football League.

Mr. and Mrs. Edward Holt had invited the team to their home after this particular game for food and fellowship. Their late son, John, was one of our students at ASD and he was so excited about our coming to his home. He had requested that his mother make his favorite chocolate cake that she made with mayonnaise instead of butter or shortening. It was a great evening—a typical Saturday night benefit game and fellowship. It was special and so was John.

CELEBTITY CLASSIC

The annual Celebrity Basketball Classic was one of the bigger benefit games in Arkansas. It seemed the Nutt brothers were always a part of that and there was always a packed house.

The 1991 Celebrity Classic was to benefit the athletic program. Many basketball stars from around the state of Arkansas were there. To name a few: Marvin Delph, a member of the famed Razorback "triplets," along with Sidney Moncrief and Ron Brewer. Others were Quinn Grovey, quarterback at the University of Arkansas; Tracy Steele, Rice University; Terry Nelson, L.A. Rams, starting tight-end in Super Bowl XIV; and Dennis Nutt, T.C.U./Dallas Mavericks, and the only one of our four sons able to be there.

It was a night for the stars and in case anyone was counting, that little gym was packed to the max and then some. The Sparkman, Ark. athletic program was greatly benefited.

The Nutt Brothers Team. Back row: Houston Nutt, Fay Nutt, Don Martin, John Williams, and Gordon Hornaday. Front row: David Poole, Wallace Tedder, Tony Morganshire, and Clyde Nutt.

GETTING YOUR MONEY'S WORTH

The Nutt brothers also exhibited some Globetrotters' tricks during each game. Houston Sr. was mostly the "trickster." He wanted the people to get their money's worth.

The brothers would fast break down the court. They always knew the where-a-bouts of each other on the court. They would pass the ball while looking the other way. The ball was invariably caught and put through the hoop. They were entertaining, to say the least.

Houston had a favorite trick he did at least once in every game. During fast break, he would slip the ball between his legs and throw his hands up as if making a shot. As the opponents looked for the ball, Houston easily put the ball through the hoop. The spectators would go wild! And yes, the people got their money's worth!

HOUSTON WAS AHEAD OF THE TIMES

As several have mentioned earlier, Houston was ahead of his time playing and handling the basketball and he could have been ahead of his time in another area as well.

In the early 60s, before AAU was big or perhaps even existed, Houston was gathering his little team of boys and traveling all over the state of Arkansas. The men's opposing team would have a young team ready to play our Pee Wee team.

The Nutt Pee Wee game was the real attraction every Saturday night—according to the moms anyway. Other than our sons and cousins, there might be any of the following boys on any given Saturday night: Jerry Belew, Roger Spratlin, Robin Cline, Herren Hickingbotham and maybe one or two Carter boys.

Our boys so looked forward to these games. They would have their bags packed long before time to leave, checking and re-checking, making sure they had their uniforms, socks and both tennis shoes. We traveled all over the state to play these games. Sometimes there would be a caravan of cars making the trip.

There were no cell phones, and messages were often conveyed via sign language. The boys would sign "eat," "restroom"—whatever the need, and someone in the car ahead or behind would deliver the message. The boys thought sign language was pretty cool.

Most Saturday nights after the games, we would get home at midnight or even later. Houston would carry the boys into the house one by one, sound asleep, and lay them on the floor. While he brought in all the gear, I would fix the bath water and literally walk each one to the tub, asleep. When the last one was bathed and in bed, Houston's last words of instruction would be, "Let the boys sleep in the morning." I always followed his instructions—but those I could not because it involved missing church. We played every Saturday night and they couldn't miss church the whole basketball season.

Come Sunday morning, although the boys were very tired and half asleep, we made it to breakfast, got dressed, grabbed Bibles, offerings, and we were off to Sunday school.

"As unto the bow the cord is, so unto man is woman, she bends him yet she follows; unless each without the other." - Henry Wadsworth Longfellow.

The traveling and playing in those Pee Wee games served a two-fold purpose: while basketball skills were being improved, charities were supported.

The era of charity games, including Pee Wee, games was our way of life for more than a decade and those memories are most treasured.

Houston's Pee Wee Team

Jr. Deputy League - 1970

CHAPTER 8

THE BENNIE FULLER ERA; 1965-1971

I n the mid '60s a phenomenal player surfaced, which may happen once in a lifetime, if at all. For this to happen at the Arkansas School for the Deaf was huge! Bennie Fuller literally put ASD on the map and made Houston a great coach. It was very exciting to coach a player like Bennie and the joy lasted a lifetime.

Bennie and the school were recognized nationally and everyone in the state knew him or at least knew of him because of the press and his basketball prowess. He was all the talk in the sports world. Wherever we went, people were talking about him and he is still talked about today. It was a great time for the deaf school, the coach and the teams to follow.

BENNIE FULLER'S BIO

Bennie Fuller is one of seven children born to Mr. and Mrs. Tammie Fuller of Hensley, Arkansas. He has three brothers and three sisters. When he was seven years old he started to school at the Madison Street School for the Deaf in Little Rock, which was officially named the Arkansas School for the Colored Deaf and Blind.

> "In 1950, the 'colored' department was moved off the ASD campus to a newer and larger facility on 21st and Madison Streets. This new facility provided for the blind as well as the deaf. The history of Madison

School ended in 1965 with the integration of black students on the campus of ASD." - *Still I Rise* by Dr. Glen Anderson.

Houston and Bennie

INTEGRATION IN BENNIE'S FAVOR

The students at the Madison School were integrated with the students at the Arkansas School for the Deaf on Markham Street in 1965. Houston was very happy to have these students on our campus because he had more ball players. This was great for our athletic programs.

With the merging of the schools, Houston met Bennie Fuller for the first time, and that was the beginning of a life-long relationship. He was very impressed with Bennie's talent and how well he could shoot the ball. By the time he became a freshman, Bennie was 6 foot 2 inches, 185 pounds and was beginning to be recognized.

Bennie Fuller (#10) in Junior High, Coach Nutt, kneeling

Bennie Fuller (#24) in High School, coach Nutt, kneeling

FULLER FILLS GYMNASIUMS

During Bennie Fuller's high school days, he was filling gymnasiums over the state of Arkansas and ASD was no exception. When Bennie played at home, our gym was overflowing and people were turned away. Fans would gather outside and try to look through the windows. It was very clear the old gym in Parnell Hall no longer met our needs.

Houston reserved seats for state legislators to attend a special home game. After seeing this firsthand, they realized it was time for the Arkansas School for the Deaf to have a new gym. Two of our legislators, Lacy Landers from Benton and Bobby Newman from Smackover, were instrumental in appropriating funds for the new gym.

BENNIE WOWS THE CROWD WITH 102 POINTS!

Bennie poured in an unbelievable 102 points to lead his team past Leola, 133 - 58. People asked how he did it. He had 22 points in the first quarter, 22 in the second and 20 in the third. Then he really banged away with 38 in the fourth.

One reporter said, "Coach, tell me about Bennie." Houston replied, "He doesn't try any fancy stuff like passing behind his back—Pete Maravich style. Bennie gets his shots when he's on the move. He passes the ball and his teammates throw it right back to him, then he takes that jump shot and its two points. He's a good shooter—fast, real quick, a great passer and he can dribble with either hand." Coach Nutt called it, 'the greatest performance I've ever seen by a high school player.'" - *Arkansas Democrat* January 20, 1971

ONE'S AMUSEMENT IS ANOTHER'S DILEMMA

One afternoon when we were in a Little Rock bank, a man who appeared to be very serious approached Houston. Pointing outside, he said, "Did you know that famous player of yours got hit by a car?" Almost in a panic, Houston immediately sprinted toward the door, not hearing the man yell that he was only teasing and was apologizing repeatedly. I was concerned what might happen next. Needless to say, that didn't set well with Houston!

ALL-STAR GAME

Bennie was named to the All-Star team his senior year. They practiced at the University of Central Arkansas the week preceding the game, although it was played at Barton Coliseum in Little Rock.

Houston would eagerly check the newspaper every morning, but not one word about Bennie could be found in the newspaper. It was Wednesday and he was beginning to worry. He told me, "I'm going to Conway to see about Bennie."

After Houston's visit with the coach, Bennie was allowed to play in his familiar position as point or shooting guard. In the All-Star game, he made 28 points and was named MVP. If Houston had not gone to Conway to check on him, he very likely would not have played. (See Appendix 14.)

THE CAMDEN-FAIRVIEW EXHIBITION GAME

During Bennie Fuller's senior year, 1971, Houston received an invitation from Coach Pat Foster inviting the Deaf School to Camden-Fairview to play a game. Coach Foster thought he had a guard who could take care of Bennie Fuller. After the game, he admitted the stories he had heard about Bennie were true.

These invitational games were special. Not only were the games played before large crowds but the ride home in the old yellow school bus was more enjoyable as well. The reason being—it was not the usual sack lunch of bologna and an apple. The team was treated to hamburgers and French fries. That was big in those days! Stories about this particular game were often told and there were many versions, depending on who was telling it.

Unexpectedly, during a sad occasion in 2003, while sitting with our dear, grieving friends in a guest room at the Baptist Medical

Center in Little Rock, Buddy Sutton, with his keen sense of humor, said, "Now that we have Rex Horne and Houston Nutt in the same room, we're going to pin them down and see who's telling the truth." He was, of course, referring to the Camden-Fairview/Deaf School game. Everyone in the room laughed; however, no one offered any information. Once again, an atmosphere of reverence and sadness prevailed.

As you see, this Camden-Fairview Invitational game is still talked about today and, once again, the game was brought up during a certain conversation.

When Bennie Fuller fouled out during this particular game, a time-out was called so the coaching staff could explain that since the fans had filled the gymnasium to see Bennie play and the game did not count in conference play, would it not be good to let Bennie finish the game? The refs agreed.

There is still another point of interest about this game: Houston would have never dreamed that one of Pat Foster's Fairview Cardinals would one day be his pastor at Immanuel Baptist Church in Little Rock. It was wonderful having Dr. Rex Horne as our pastor and one year before his tenure of 16 years ended, he preached Houston's funeral.

The Camden-Fairview game will always be remembered and talked about for all kinds of different reasons—and Buddy, we may never know the truth about it!

Making it official

Bennie signs for Pensacola Junior College as Coach Nutt, Bennie's mother and Jim Atkinson, head basketball coach at Pensacola Junior College, look on

Bennie as an All-Star

Bennie (at left) smiles as his coach, Houston, praises him for a special commendation given to him for his outstanding basketball achievements by the state House of Representatives.

A HOUSE RESOLUTION

A Resolution was introduced in the Arkansas State House of Representatives on February 2, 1971, in honor of Bennie Fuller, commending him for his outstanding sportsmanship and scoring record as a member of the Arkansas School for the Deaf basketball team. (See Appendix 15.)

SCORING AVERAGE

His 50.9 scoring average was the nation's highest among high school basketball players, and his 102 points scored in a single game was the second highest ever in high school history. He holds the all-time school records for the most points scored in one season: 1,347 and his four-year point total—4,261. He was the most talked about player in Arkansas since Almer Lee in 1968.

ASD GETS NATIONAL ATTENTION

With all the national attention swirling around the Arkansas School for the Deaf, Bennie Fuller's senior year was a very exciting time. As I recall, this was the first time our school had been given national attention because of a student athlete. The scholarship inquiries for Bennie were pouring in from major schools: Florida State, Kansas, Nebraska, Oklahoma State, Arkansas, Tennessee, and others.

College coaches were visiting our campus and the phone was ringing off the wall—we didn't have e-mails or cell phones then. The scouts were impressed with what they saw in Bennie, but they really didn't understand the academics that were necessary for him. They were just thinking of him as a player on their team. He would have done well on any of them.

It was a big job for Houston to keep Bennie and his parents informed of all the scholarship offers and the interest surrounding him. Bennie had no idea of the enormity of his situation; however, he took it all in stride and stayed humble during the whole process.

Bennie was working toward a printing apprenticeship and not many colleges offered that. His parents were very proud of his basketball skills and appreciative for the opportunity to go to college. Houston, the parents and Bennie carefully checked out each of the colleges and tried to choose the one that best suited him.

BENNIE ACCEPTS SCHOLARSHIP

Bennie accepted a scholarship from Pensacola Junior College, Pensacola, Florida. After the two years of college was completed there, Bennie finished up at UAPB in Pine Bluff, Arkansas. Following his college career, he tried out with the Phoenix Suns. There were practices and scrimmage games, but you have to know how difficult that was for him without interpreters. Neither the coach nor the players could talk to Bennie and he couldn't hear a word that was being said around him. The only way to communicate was to use pen and paper. After a challenging year, he decided it was time to go home, get a job and be with his family.

BASKETBALL COURT NAMED IN BENNIE'S HONOR

On January 12, 2013, the basketball court at the Nutt Athletic Complex was christened as the Bennie Fuller Court.

There were funny stories, gifts and deserving speeches in the old gym where Bennie played. Friends and family were treated to a barbeque luncheon catered by Corky's Barbeque. The final ceremony of the day was in the Nutt Athletic Complex preceding the ASD homecoming game.

The question was asked, "What would Houston Sr. think?" He would be very pleased! It is most appropriate that the court bear Bennie Fuller's name. After all, it was his basketball prowess, as well as Houston Sr.'s hard work, that enabled us to have the new gym at ASD.

Bennie was employed at the United States Post Office in Oklahoma City for 28 years and retired on January 30, 2013.

BENNIE'S HONORS AND AWARDS

- Deaf Prep Basketball Player of the year 1970;
- Most Valuable Player in the Cabot Invitational Tournament 1969-1970 and 1970-1971;
- Worthen Sports Award for Arkansas - March 1971;
- BC Scouting and Coaches All-American;
- Top 60 Player All-Southern Team;
- Sunkist All-American - 1971; and
- Deaf Athlete of the Year - 1971.

Bennie was inducted into the Arkansas Sports Hall of Fame on February 28, 2014.

Bennie and his wife, the former Emma Brown, reside in Oklahoma City. They have four children and six grandchildren.

CHAPTER 9

HOUSTON'S LAST GAMES
AND RETIREMENT

AUSTIN CLASSIC - 1986

Following the Bennie Fuller Era, the school did survive and win victories. Houston and his assistant, the late Coach Grady Berry, took the ASD basketball team to Austin, Texas, for a tournament at the Texas School for the Deaf. It was special because all the teams were deaf. There is much enthusiasm and anticipation when deaf teams play other deaf teams because they feel such confidence. They feel at a disadvantage when playing hearing teams. For example, if the deaf person doesn't see the open man, he misses the easy shot, while the hearing person can let his teammates know that he's open under the basket.

After all the tours and social gatherings were over, it was time for the tournament play. We won our first game against Louisiana, the second game against Oklahoma, and it was down to Texas in the championship game!

Houston took those games seriously and could motivate his players *"to the hilt!" It didn't matter that the Texas school was a much larger team than ours and that they were a good team. As mentioned earlier, I can still see the knuckles on the back of Houston's hands turning white as he signed so forcefully, "You can BEAT them, because you're

---

* to the hilt - completely

better!" with emphasis on the word BEAT, as right "S" hand placed over left "S " hand moves over and down, with a determined look on his face that no one could overlook!

I couldn't believe it! We beat Texas 52-42! That was HUGE!

Houston was so proud of this team, and said, "They all deserve a trophy!" The team and coaches were feeling an all-time "Victory High," and part of the celebration was cutting down the net!

They not only took home the first-place trophy, but they had the opportunity to tour the Texas State Capitol and the L.B.J. Presidential Library!

If the students were asked about the championship game or the tours, they would quickly flash the sign "Finish Touch!" This expression is used in a situation when you have been there and/or have done that. Indeed, the school won victories after the Bennie Fuller Era, even a championship game—"Yes, Finish Touch!"

PHOTOGRAPHY BY KELLY HERRELL

Basketball champions at the Texas School for the Deaf Invitational Tournament. Front row: Fred Pickett, Philip Wilson and Emmit Dansby. Back row: Grady Berry, assistant coach, Leroy Robinson, Jamie Harper, Ronny Calhoun, Norman Holloway, Leon Williams, and Coach Houston Nutt

Cutting down the net

A FORMER ASD STUDENT

Betty Bounds, one of our former students at ASD, was teacher, principal and assistant superintendent at the Texas School for the Deaf, 1994-2007.

In the spring of 2004, Houston Sr. and I flew to Austin and Dennis met us at the airport. He was to be the guest speaker at the All-Sports Banquet that evening at the school. Upon our arrival, Betty gave us a grand tour of the campus. At that time Dennis was men's basketball coach at Texas State, which is only about 45 minutes from TSD. The coach, who incidentally was deaf, had taken his players to Dennis' basketball camps in San Marcos and he and Dennis had become friends.

It was a great evening and it is always gratifying to see your former students doing well, especially as a teacher of the deaf. Equally gratifying is seeing your son interacting with the deaf and reaching back into his heritage, as he carries out his father's legacy. (Betty Bounds is now retired.)

HOUSTON'S LAST GAME AT ASD

Houston's last game was in December 1987 and Susan Pack, the superintendent at ASD, had planned a surprise for him. She had sent word for me to be sure to be there for the surprise. I never dreamed of anything more.

At halftime, the superintendent, former students and players congregated to the center of the basketball court. Houston and I joined them. In addition to the normal crowd, two of our State Representatives, Bobby Newman, Lacy Landers and wife, Lee, and our son, Dickey, were in attendance. We still had no idea what was about to happen.

The chairman of the board, Mr. Race Drake, along with his interpreter, walked to the middle of the basketball court and explained the reason we were all gathered there. Everyone knew except Houston and me. When he got the crowd's attention, he made a few brief remarks and then said:

> "On behalf of the board of trustees at the Arkansas Schools for the Deaf and Blind, the gymnasium will be named the Nutt Athletic Complex to honor Houston and Emogene Nutt, who gave unselfishly a combined 62 years of service to the students of the Arkansas School for the Deaf."

This was totally unexpected and, of course, we were very surprised. Mr. Drake showed the audience a plaque that would be placed on the wall in the gymnasium. He then presented us with a framed picture of the new gymnasium and two gallon jars filled with the money that was collected at the door. I remember thinking—*"what more could there be?"*

Lacy Landers and Bobby Newman were not only instrumental in appropriating funds to build the new gymnasium but made sure the plans were carried out. Bobby Newman served in the Arkansas House of Representatives 1969-1998, and Lacy Landers served as State Representative for 32 years, including Speaker of the House. They were always ready and willing to do anything they could for the Arkansas School for the Deaf during their time of service to the state.

When Houston was asked in an interview what he thought about the honor, he said, "I am a little worried, because I thought you were supposed to be dead before a building was named for you."

Arkansas School for the Deaf

Nutt Athletic Complex

In honor of Houston and Emogene Nutt,
who gave unselfishly a combined 61 years of service
to the students of the Arkansas School for the Deaf.

December 15, 1987

Nutt Athletic Complex

Team members congratulating Houston and Emogene

Left to Right – Lacy Landers, Emogene, Houston and Bobby Newman

Houston and Emogene accept Plaque

THE NEW GYM

The new gymnasium on the ASD campus was wonderful! The construction was begun in 1975 and completed in 1977. It has a swimming pool, weight room, recreation room, classrooms, offices, dressing rooms with showers, trophy showcases and a nice basketball court. Compared to our old gym it was huge with a seating capacity of 2,500. The seats pull out from the walls for games and fold back when not in use. Houston was so proud of the new gym and he kept it so clean! We would not have been surprised had he asked us to take off our shoes before entering!

HONORS ARE A REMINDER

Calvin Coolidge said, "No person was ever honored for what he received. Honor has been the reward for what he gave."

- 1969 National Deaf Basketball Coach of the Year;
- 1985 AAAD Hall of Fame;
- 1996 Meritorious Service Award;
- 1997 Arkansas School for the Deaf Hall of Fame;

- 1997 Arkansas High School Hall of Fame; and
- 1998 A Great Friend to Children, presented by The Children's Museum of Arkansas.

Speakers for this event were: The late Paul Eells, KATV Channel 7 Sports; U.S. Senator David Pryor; Ray Tucker, Executive Director of the Arkansas Sports Hall of Fame; our pastor, Reverend Rex Horne; State Representative Bobby Newman; Dr. Steven Cathey, neurosurgeon, and his wife, Dr. Janet Cathy, gynecologist, who served jointly as chairpersons of Great Friend to Children.

The late Paul Eells did his homework and came up with this story:

> "There were frequent visits with family at Fordyce, and there was a place between Fordyce and Little Rock that had five hamburgers for a dollar. If the boys were on good behavior, Houston would stop and order five hamburgers and a Coke with six straws."

As you can imagine, he stole the show with that story.

- 2001 Arkansas Sports Hall of Fame;
- 2002 Salute to Greatness: Martin Luther King Community Service Award;
- Posthumously: 2005 Arkansas Ability Awards – Commissioner's Award for People with Disabilities;
- 2005 Lifetime Achievement Award (Houston and Emogene received jointly); and
- 2008 Dallas county Sports Hall of Fame.

A ROLE MODEL

Houston not only served as a role model for the deaf children but for hundreds of hearing children and adults; although, he really was not aware of it. For example, before his death on June 7, 2000, Houston was surprised to receive this letter:

A quote in part from Jim Blankenship, a writer for the NW Arkansas edition of the *Arkansas Democrat/Gazette*:

> "Dear Coach Nutt,
>
> "Whether you know it or not, you, Brooks Robinson Sr. and a handful of others helped shape the course of my life, simply by your example and dedication to youth.
>
> "As a teenager I played numerous basketball games in your gym. Thank you for emphasizing family values.
>
> "Thank you for being a role model to a lot of people and thank you, coach, for your years of service as a teacher of basketball and so much more.
>
> "Regards, Jim Blankenship"

Letter, dated October 26, 1995, from Barbara Northup, former teacher at ASD:

> "Dear Houston,
>
> "Thank you so much for agreeing to come to my Deaf Studies class and talk to the students about yourself and Deaf sports. You were absolutely wonderful! The students were so interested in your stories and especially about your time here at ASD. It is obvious that you love ASD and everything it stands for. Thank you for sharing that respect and love for the school with the kids.
>
> "I firmly believe that our students need to meet deaf adult role models who can make them feel proud of their deafness and develop a respect for themselves and what they can do in the future. You are an excellent role model for students here and your communication with them is outstanding.

"Again, I appreciate you for giving time out of your busy schedule to come.

"Sincerely,
"Barbara E. Northup"

After Houston's death, there were many letters, thanking him for being a role model. In 2008 I received a letter from Dr. Steve Eubanks, a family friend and our veterinarian:

"Mrs. Emogene,

"I considered Houston Nutt Sr. one of my very best friends and truly an example for any father to follow. Few people knew the closeness and true friendship that he and I enjoyed.

"He was inspiring to me and always eager to praise, yet the side I admired the most about him was that he had no problem in calling me down.

"Houston Sr. had a way of inspiring young men. He inspired me and always made me feel like I was one of his boys.

"Thanks for continuing that tradition by making me and my family part of your family.

"Thanks again, Dr. Steve"

HOUSTON NUTT LEFT A BIG MARK - was the headline to a story in the *Arkansas Gazette* on March 30, 1988. In part, it read:

> "As coach, athletic director, and dean of students, Houston made a significant contribution to the deaf students at the Arkansas School for the Deaf, but that was a small part compared to the mark made by the "intangibles.""

In 1998, Houston was honored by being selected as "A Great Friend to Children," by The Children's Museum of Arkansas, as the person in the community, who had made major contributions to the growth and positive development of children—with this recognition:

> "The encouragement, self-esteem and values he has imparted to them are the 'intangible' benefits of his efforts that have a lasting, positive influence."

Living two and a half blocks from the deaf school for almost three decades made it possible for Houston to spend a lot of time on campus. The boys at the school would see his car and run to the gym, then another and another. They were content just to sit in his office while he did paper work or they would ask if they could do something— empty waste baskets, sweep the gym floor or straighten the dressing rooms—anything. Just hanging around and being associated with someone with whom they could identify was a confidence builder.

"Houston's demeanor is not what you may think, but rather proud," said Larry Lacewell, former Director of Scouting for the Dallas Cowboys. Lacewell grew up in Fordyce and knew Houston and the family very well.

While Houston was coaching the deaf, he also coached football, baseball and basketball in the Little Leagues, as mentioned earlier. We couldn't go out to eat or anywhere else for that matter, without someone saying, "Coach Nutt, do you remember me?" Of course he didn't every time because they were grown men with families.

Houston not only left a big mark at the deaf school, but he also influenced hundreds of young boys in the community through Little League, YMCA and Boys Club.

ATTACHED TO ASD FOR LIFE

From birth to death, Houston Sr. was attached in some way to the Arkansas School for the Deaf. In addition to his father, uncles, aunt, and brothers who attended the Arkansas School for the Deaf, he also attended the school for a short time. Later he returned and stayed more than three decades as a teacher and coach.

In retirement he was appointed to serve on the Arkansas School for the Deaf and Blind Board of Trustees where he was serving his third term at the time of his death. He was appointed to serve his first term by Governor Jim Guy Tucker and by Governor Mike Huckabee to the second and third terms. The late Judge Eliza Jane Roy, a dear friend, administered the oath.

One could say he gave his whole life to the deaf and, yes, he indeed left a big mark at the Arkansas School for the Deaf.

> *"Happy are those who respect the Lord and obey him. You will enjoy what you work for, and you will be blessed with good things. Your wife will give you many children, like a vine that produces much fruit. Your children will bring you much good, like olive branches that produce many olives. This is how the man who respects the Lord will be blessed"* (Psalms 128:1 – Devotional Bible – NCV by Max Lucado).

RETIREMENT

In 1987 Governor Bill Clinton introduced an Early Incentive Retirement Program, supposedly to save the state money; however, so many people took advantage of it, I'm not sure it did! There were several provisions, and the applicable one for us was having been teachers with 30 or more years in the state system. Houston and I had 31 years of service, so we took advantage of this offer. It was a huge step for both of us to leave the school and the work that was very dear to our hearts—almost 10 years before we had planned.

If we retired, we'd have to move from that neighborhood because our house was only two and a half blocks from the school, and the kids would be knocking on the front door, expecting Houston to solve their problems. Secondly, our home at 311 Rice was where all of our sons were born, except for Houston Dale, and they had grown up on the deaf school campus, which was their second home. We had lived there almost 30 years and it was there that all the childhood memories were accumulated.

House at 311 Rice

In spite of mixed emotions, my last day was at the close of the school year—June 1987. Houston stayed until the end of the year so he could coach his junior and senior teams through December.

After much discussion, we retired and moved; however, any time the boys come home, even if dinner is waiting, first, they drive by 311 Rice and the Arkansas School for the Deaf.

Retirement was wonderful! Our first grandson was born in March 1987, and in the following nine years there would be a total of 13 grandchildren. In case the math doesn't add up, there were two sets of twins and one set of triplets born during those nine years.

The last family picture with Houston, July 4, 2001

CHAPTER 10

HOUSTON'S CLOSING CHAPTER

At the dawn of the 21st century, Houston Sr. was doing great! He had lost excess weight and his blood pressure was very good. He felt so good and looked as if he would live forever.

Four of our grandchildren were playing AAU ball in Little Rock on the same weekend as the Red and White Game in Fayetteville. We chose to stay home and watch the grandchildren's games. There was nothing Houston enjoyed more and, as it turned out, that was his last weekend here on earth. Before the weekend was over, I think we had watched games in just about every gymnasium in Little Rock. He could not have lived a weekend more fully nor could he have enjoyed anything more. It was a great weekend!

We were anticipating a normal Monday morning. Instead, Houston woke me up at 4 a.m. with numbness in his right arm. He got out of bed and walked down the hall to the living room to sit in his recliner, as he often did, but this time he soon called for me. As I hurried down the hall, I heard him say, "Something is wrong," as he picked up his arm and let it drop lifelessly, "I'm having a stroke, call someone!" I called 911 immediately.

While I was on the phone, he sat in his chair and began pleading with God. *"Please, please. No, God! I don't want to be like my dad. No, no, God!"* His father had suffered a stroke and lived eight years with paralysis and Houston did not want that. The pleading lasted a while and then, unexpectedly, it stopped. He was staring straight ahead in dead silence. The lady on the phone asked me if Houston was conscious. I was patting his cheeks and talking to him frantically. No, he was not conscious and he never regained consciousness. God answered his prayer.

The 911 crew arrived and transported Houston by ambulance to the Baptist Medical Center. The doctors were very caring and did everything possible to make us comfortable.

My neighbor sat with me until the boys could get there. Houston Dale flew in from Fayetteville, while Dickey luckily de-boarded a plane in Memphis before takeoff and drove to Little Rock. Danny drove in from Hot Springs where he was recruiting and Dennis flew in from San Marcos, Texas.

After reviewing the CT scan and MRI, they told us Houston Sr. had had a massive stroke and did not expect him to regain consciousness. At the same time, they assured us that he never felt any pain. He was placed in a special ward and the nurses were very considerate to allow us to go in as often and stay as long as we wanted. He lived three days.

Sometimes we would hold his hand and reminisce. On one occasion Dennis said, "Look, dad's fingers are positioned to say, 'I love you,' in sign language." Each time we went in the room to be with him it was a quiet and prayerful observation, as if it were a vigil, watching over him as he slept.

Then it was down to those final minutes. We reverently and prayerfully surrounded his bed, as we watched the heart monitor slowly move across the screen. The only audible thing in the room was the inhalation and exhalation of Houston's breathing; yet, each had his or her own personal thoughts as we watched quietly.

My thoughts flashed back to Houston's near-death experience when he had his first heart attack in 1991. He didn't want that experience to end. Again and again he would say in sign language as well as voice: "Everything was a beautiful blue. It was so beautiful, I can't describe it—and I could hear! I want to stay just like that." I thought, Houston is about to experience that 'beautiful blue,' as well as Dr. Vaught's often spoken words of transition, "... *absent from the body and present with the Lord*" (II Cor. 5:8 - NKJV). As the heart rate continued to decrease, we stood around his bed, motionlessly and reverently, with eyes following each mark across the screen:

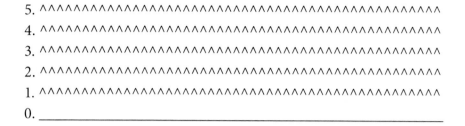

5. ∧∧

4. ∧∧

3. ∧∧

2. ∧∧

1. ∧∧

0. _____

That final flat line made its way across the screen at 2:38 p.m., April 20th, 2005. Houston had "... *fought the good fight, finished the race, and kept the faith*" (II Timothy 4:7 – NKJV).

As some would say, Houston's whole life here on earth has been associated with ballgames, losses and victories, and now—an eternal victory. "... *Death has been swallowed up in victory*" (I Cor. 15:54 – NIV).

> "*Everyone who competes in the games goes into strict training. They do it to get a crown that will not last; but we do it to get a crown that will last forever*" (I Cor. 9:25 – NIV).

The news of Houston's death spread fast via radio and television. CNN scrolled these words across the bottom of the screen: "*Houston Nutt, Sr. has died, his four sons are college coaches.*"

There were many stories in the *Arkansas Democrat-Gazette* about his death. One story on the editorial page especially touched my heart and I quote in part from an editorial on Friday, April 22, 2005:

HOUSTON NUTT, SR
THE ORIGINAL COACH NUTT

> "On that frost-bitten Turkey Day, Central High was playing Hall High. This game became our traditional Turkey Day game. Every year it seemed as if the

Tigers had the same quarterback, some strong-armed, fundamentally sound, hotshot named Nutt. Following Houston there was Dickey Nutt, Danny Nutt and Dennis Nutt. Would it ever end?

"My dad knew all about these Nutts. He knew the original Nutt Brothers, those barnstorming basketball players who always seemed to find a game and draw a crowd. And nobody who knew the first Houston was not the least bit surprised at the way all these little Nutts just kept-a-comin' and going on to play college ball. And no one who knew the first Houston was surprised that all his boys went into coaching either.

"When the news of Houston Sr.'s passing was received, those *Arkansas Gazette* and *Arkansas Democrat* stories came rushing back.

"There was Houston Nutt, Sr.'s last game coaching the basketball team at the Arkansas School for the Deaf. The *Arkansas Democrat* covered it miraculously. We could picture Coach Nutt in action - signing to his players, working the refs, living and dying with each possession as if the national championship were at stake. We wondered then how a man still so passionate could give that up, even after more than three decades. As we got older, we came to understand. Houston Nutt, Sr. didn't give up his passion. He passed it on. He passed it on to his 4 sons—to Houston Dale who coaches football at the University of Arkansas. He passed it on to Dickey who coaches basketball at Arkansas State. He passed it on to Danny who coaches the Razorback running backs. He passed it on to Dennis who coaches basketball at Texas State.

"In a way, Houston Nutt, Sr. passed on his passion to the whole lot of us.... Arkansas is still small enough to be family.... Lots of times we feel brotherly and sisterly even towards folks we only know by name and reputation and long familiar history, like the Nutts. Yes, we'll miss having Houston Nutt, Sr. in the family. We'll miss dad."

Thank you *Arkansas Democrat/Gazette* for allowing me to use this story. It touched my heart as you unfolded the whole life of Houston Sr.

YOU'RE THE BEST!

You're The Best!
Drawing by Luis (11 years old), a student at ASD

Houston Sr. will be remembered by his signature phrase, "You're the Best!" No one can sign it quite like he did. He would sign, "You're The Best," then turn to me and say, "Emogene, tell them what I said." Thinking *"Oh no!"* and as best as I could, I would tell them, "You're the best!" And to my surprise, their faces would light up immediately! That stranger's solemn face would be transformed into smiles, and before leaving you would have thought they had been best friends forever.

> *"Remember to welcome strangers because some who have done this have welcomed angels without knowing it"* (Hebrews 13: 2 - Devotional Bible - NCV by Max Lucado).

One night after Houston's death, Dickey went to the grocery store for milk. A young African-American male, who was sacking groceries, insisted on carrying out the milk for Dickey. By the time they walked to the car and set the milk down he had completed his story about Houston. To sum it up, Houston made him feel special by always telling him, "You're the Best!" He signed that phrase to everyone and everyone loved it.

SAYING "GOODBYE"

Houston's memorial service was held at our beloved Immanuel Baptist Church in Little Rock. Our pastor and friend, Dr. Rex Horne, conducted the service. He summed up Houston's life in such a wonderful way that I would like to share it with my readers.

Dr. Horne said he chose this Scripture about a game or competition that reminds us of Houston:

> "*Therefore since we are surrounded by such a great cloud of witnesses, let us throw off everything that hinders and the sin that so easily entangles, and let us run with perseverance the race marked out for us*" (Hebrews 12:1 – NIV).

He began: "**Let us run the race with purpose**: Houston was a straight arrow, focused, moral, and direct. Houston may not always be right but he was never in doubt. Not a lazy step allowed. The boys practiced as if practicing for a championship. He was hard on them, because he wanted them to be the best."

"**Let us run with pride**: Houston's pride was rooted in love. Emogene, your boys know, your church family knows, we all know that outside of Houston accepting Jesus as his Savior—the best decision he ever made was to marry you."

He continued, "Houston had pride in his sons, Houston Dale, Dickey, Danny and Dennis and he was proud of their work as college coaches."

He also told that story that gets told so often about Houston Sr. sitting on Row 15, getting Dickey's attention and communicating in sign language, *Why is number 25 not in the game?*

Dr. Horne continued by saying, "He had pride in his grandchildren. How he loved his grandchildren. The boys have always said dad could never have handled a daughter. It is ironic that 10 of those grandchildren are granddaughters. They were loved just as the three grandsons and the reason Hanna sang at Houston's memorial service was his last words to her, 'Hanna, next time you sing, I want to be there!' Dr. Horne reminded us that Houston did know how to handle them—he loved them. Houston had pride in his daughters-in-law. He was proud of them all."

He mentioned another kind of pride, and that was Houston's working with the deaf. "How he loved the deaf. Working with the deaf was his ambition and joy. He worked long hours spilling over into weekends for over 30 years. During retirement, his work continued with the deaf as he was appointed to serve on the Arkansas School for the Deaf and Blind Board of Trustees. He was serving his third term at the time of his death."

Dr. Horne continued: "**Let us prepare**: Houston prepared his family by facing his own challenge. He prepared his family by where he worked, by where he lived and where he worshiped. They didn't live in the most desired place. They were taught that social status doesn't matter, color of skin doesn't matter, the Person matters. The four boys grew up to be college coaches. Houston prepared them well."

The service was closed with a letter that I wrote on the night of Houston's death. I couldn't sleep, so I got up and wrote this letter to him:

"Dear Houston,
"When I first met you, you were tall, thin—and handsome!! The first thing out of your mouth was, "Do you know me?" My reply was, "No, I don't know you." You replied, "Well... I played ball for Adolph Rupp in Kentucky and now I'm playing basketball for Hank Iba." I WAS NOT IMPRESSED!!!
"As time went on, I WAS impressed because...you never smoked, never drank and you were a Christian.

"You brought me to Arkansas...into a world of DEAF culture...I couldn't understand a word that was said! I often asked God, "What am I doing here?" But, I made it through. You gave me four wonderful sons! You disciplined them in such a way...all I had to do was say, "Do you want me to tell Daddy?" Some say they look like you, walk like you and some say they even 'act' like you! They all have followed in your footsteps...knowing well the long hours and hard work involved. I know you are proud of them...I am, too.

"We have already missed you so much! You know you could never keep up with me... and I keep looking back for you!

"Oh, by the way... please tell Jesus that the woman who is always praying for her sons' games is your wife.

"One more thing... please do not "BRAG" on the grandkids too much. He already knows more about them than you do. He knows 'little' Houston is so tall...strong and is quarterback for his high school team and what a good player Hailey is...and how well Hanna can sing! Haven is a player too, WOW!

"He already knows how Logan breaks all records in basketball and football...and that Luke has grown so tall and...can he shoot the "three!" and Lexis is so sweet and grown-up. Then there's Dallas who tumbles, plays ball... and the triplets, Ashley, Brenna and Caylan are into basketball.

"He already knows all about Myca and Macy's soccer team and basketball. But, if you must BRAG... almost all 13 grandchildren have accepted Jesus as their Lord and Savior!!!

"We all love you and miss you. We're so proud for you and NEVER again will you have to say....'Emogene, what did he say?' I know you are surprised to hear the birds 'singing' so beautifully! We love you very much, and the boys will try hard to carry on your legacy!

"With love,

"Your wife (for 49 years), sons, daughters-in-law and grandchildren.

"P.S. Please stand near the Golden Gates so you will be the first one to greet us!

"Love you!"

Family without Houston Sr., 2008

CHAPTER 11

HOUSTON REMEMBERED

The following letters were received after Houston Sr.'s death:

MIKE HUCKABEE*

Dear Nutt Family,

The death of Houston, Sr. is a loss felt most by your family, but shared deeply with all the people of Arkansas.

Some people leave memories; others leave lasting legacies. He leaves a true legacy of an authentic faith in Christ, a servant's heart, thousands of lives touched and changed by his years as a coach and an educator and perhaps his greatest legacy, that of a family upon whom the imprint of his character is indelibly stamped.

I am not only indebted to him for his many kindnesses toward Janet and me, but I especially cherish how kind and thoughtful he was to our son David.

One of my greatest memories as Governor is the wonderful service honoring Mr. Nutt at the Twin Lakes Baptist Church in Mountain Home. The tribute was not only touching, but was a wonderful testimony to godly manhood and true fatherhood. What a role model for all fathers!

---

* Mike Huckabee served as Governor of Arkansas from 1996 to 2007

Thank you for sharing him with so many of us. His service to our state will live on through the lives of those he coached, taught, encouraged, or simply smiled at and made feel special.

With Christian sympathy,
Mike Huckabee, Governor of Arkansas

DAVID PRYOR*

There are few (if any) Arkansas families that have made a greater contribution to athletics and the spirit of real sportsmanship than the Nutt family. Even as far back as the Sam Coleman Camden Panther days, I had the good fortune of competing with Houston Sr. when he quarterbacked the Fordyce Redbugs. He and his gallant family have touched and inspired literally thousands of young people—including my three sons.

Arkansas has been fortunate indeed to have produced a family like the Nutts. They have compassion, class and a real sense of purpose.

With gratitude,
David Pryor
U.S. Senator

JACK GRESHAM

MY MEMORY OF HOUSTON

My memories of Houston date back to those days he starred in basketball and football at Fordyce High School. He was a magician in hiding the football on handoffs to teammates in the T formation, a new offensive plan at that time.

His basketball prowess was never equaled, before or since.

Houston's skill in athletics set him apart, but his politeness and personal good conduct held him in good stead, both on and off the court.

---

* David Pryor served three terms in the U. S. House of Representatives, Governor of the state of Arkansas, and three terms as Arkansas' U. S. Senator.

Naturally, I followed him when he went to Kentucky to play for Adolph Rupp, and later for Hank Iba at Oklahoma A&M. I continued that same interest when Houston returned to his native state to begin a long career at the Ark School for the Deaf.

The world is a better place for having had Houston Nutt fulfill his role as an athlete, as a husband and as a father. His friends and his family will miss him, to be sure, but they will not forget the contribution he made to their lives.

Sincerely with love,
Jack H. Gresham
Superintendent Fordyce High School

BOBBY NEWMAN*

A SPECIAL PERSON

I first met Houston Nutt in 1948 when he was playing basketball for the Fordyce *Redbugs*. The *Redbugs* were in a high school basketball tournament, which was being held at Ouachita Baptist College, where I was a student. Each team in the tournament had an athlete from Ouachita assigned to them to serve as their "gofer." It was my lucky day! I was assigned to the Fordyce team. Almost as soon as I met Houston I could tell there was something special about this young man, and as his life unfolded, I think everyone realized this. Houston and I formed a lifelong friendship at our first meeting and over the next 57 years, we crossed paths many times.

Houston was a good high school quarterback, a great basketball player, and a very good fast pitch softball pitcher. He was a natural athlete. The whole family was athletic, but Houston was the best athlete in the family.

Someone said Houston could watch a girl do hopscotch and the second time he would do it, he would do it better than anyone around.

---

* Bobby Newman served 30 years in the Arkansas House of Representatives. He died in 2013.

In 1969, I had the opportunity to grow closer to Houston than I had in years. He was the coach at the Arkansas School for the Deaf and I was serving my first term in the Arkansas House of Representatives. I would see Houston at the capitol, and I also visited Houston and the students (of whom he felt like were his own) numerous times at the School for the Deaf. Houston Nutt never asked for anything for himself, always someone else.

Houston loved his family. They were his pride and joy! It was a thrill for me to see Houston and his family in action. They loved the Lord and they loved each other. Houston Nutt was a legend in his own time.

Bobby G. Newman,
Arkansas House of Representatives 1969-1998

BENNIE FULLER

MY COACH

Coach Nutt Sr. was the best coach I ever had. He influenced my life in many ways. He was the best. He was also tough and he was always there for me and for all his players.

He was like a father to all of us. Coach Nutt always encouraged me, believed in me and taught me to believe in myself.

He taught me to be strong; without him I would not be the man I am today.

In closing I would like to say, Coach Nutt may be looking down from heaven with a big smile knowing what a great influence he had on my life.

Coach Nutt, I will always keep your words of encouragement in my heart and remember how you believed in me. I hope you know I love you, respect you and appreciate you for all you did for me.

Bennie Fuller
Student/basketball player at ASD

JAMES Y. SUEN, M. D.

A DIFFERENCE MAKER

It is an honor and privilege to write a few words about Houston Nutt Sr.

I want to say how much I admire Mr. Nutt, not only for being a wonderful person but the contributions he and his family have made to education and sports in the states of Arkansas and Texas.

The impact this family has made will go on and on.

All of us here at the Arkansas Cancer Research Center will never forget Mr. Nutt.

He was truly a wonderful man who made a difference in so many lives.

Sincerely,
James Y. Suen, M.D.
Executive Director, Arkansas Cancer Research Center
Professor and Chair

MARK PRYOR* RECALLS THE TIME HE LIVED WITH US AT 311 RICE IN LITTLE ROCK

Mrs. Nutt was a good cook, but the thing I remember most was her making chocolate-chip cookies. It seemed every time I went to their home, she would pull out a tin of homemade cookies. They lived at 311 Rice, which was less than three blocks from the Deaf School. Their mailbox had some sort of art design that said "The Nutts." Even though the house was modest, it was a home.

- There was an iron, spiral staircase going upstairs to Houston Dale and Dickey's room. They were away at college. I stayed there when I lived with them. They shared this large open room divided only by the staircase portal. They shared one small bathroom, but this family shared everything.

---

* Mark Pryor is the senior U. S. Senator from Arkansas

- They had a trophy case in their dining room that most high schools would envy.

- Invariably there were shoes piled by the fireplace in multiplies of four. There could be eight pairs of shoes: four pairs of basketball high tops and four pairs of football cleats.

- All six of them were funny. There was always laughter and goofing off in that house. A lot of their humor was animated and exaggerated gestures used to be better understood.

- Immanuel Baptist Church was a non-negotiable commitment on Sunday mornings.

- They were all fluent in sign language and often communicated by using sign language outside of the home. This was an advantage in some situations like sports strategy, because the other side would not know what they were up to. I remember Houston and Danny did this on the sidelines when Houston was head football coach.

- They had a basketball goal in the back yard and Mr. Nutt had welded an inner rim inside the original rim, which meant you had to be more accurate in your shooting.

- Mrs. Nutt was a saint. They drove to the ends of the earth to watch their boys play. They were constantly on the road. All four boys had a Chevrolet Camaro. Mr. Nutt bought them all used. There was a spot in front of the Little Rock Central gym, as you entered the building on 14th Street, where they would park. It seemed that no one else would dare park there, or that it was reserved for the Nutts.

- Mr. Nutt had an incredible college career. I always heard that Rupp allowed 100 players to compete for one scholarship and Mr. Nutt got it. It is unique that he played two years for Adolf Rupp at Kentucky—then transferred to Oklahoma A&M (now Oklahoma State) and played two years for the great Henry Iba.

- Mr. Nutt trained his dogs in obedience and helped Mr. Parks train his dogs.

- Mr. Nutt taught my brother, Scott, how to shoot free throws. He didn't miss after that.

- A deaf man, at one time, stayed in their back yard. I assume he was a former student and he probably would have been homeless otherwise. I think they provided meals, clothing, and money probably. I don't know what happened to him after they sold 311 Rice.

- One of our most memorable nights was when we lived in the Governor's Mansion. We had all six Nutts over for dinner and we ate in the big dining room. They were funny and so nice. Oftentimes they would "sign" details of a conversation. It was interesting because we had no idea what they were saying. It could have been "eat your peas" for all we knew. All the Pryors had a great and wonderful evening.

- My dad remembers the Nutt Brothers barnstorming around south Arkansas when he was growing up in Camden.

- When I was in law school, or maybe fresh out, I ran into Danny one day at the Little Rock Athletic Club. Naturally, he was there to play basketball. As we were warming up, we were standing beyond the 3-point line talking, laughing, shooting and enjoying each other's company. I was shooting the ball pretty well and quite a few of my 3-pointers were going in. In fact I had about the same shooting percentage as Danny and

I was feeling pretty good until I noticed Danny was shooting left handed.

- Danny had an incredibly strong arm. I saw him knock down a wide receiver one day in football practice at Little Rock Central. I also saw him play basketball at the HPER Building on the U of A campus where he routinely hit shots beyond half court.

- Dennis was amazingly quick and nimble on the basketball court. He told me, after his first practice at TCU, his shot was blocked and he realized his high school shooting motion was not going to work in the Southwest Conference, so he mastered a very quick release— so quick that you really couldn't even see it. He could set his feet and be well into his shooting motion in an instant and this made him impossible to guard. He single-handedly beat Eddie Sutton's Razorbacks one night in Barnhill Arena. All I could think of as he was unleashing his onslaught is that Eddie should have recruited him.

- In that same game, we had two very good guards who were also very good defensive players. That night, Dennis put on juke moves and "stutter" steps that literally made each one trip over themselves and fall on the floor trying to cover Dennis.

- At Forest Heights Junior High, Dennis was our best basketball player. For a pep rally, the cheerleaders wanted him to be part of a skit. He refused and refused. They begged him but he wouldn't budge. Finally they went to Coach Poole and asked him to intervene. Coach Poole said, "Dennis, if you do this, I will let you shoot as much as you want during the game." He did the skit and scored 30.

- My last story about Dennis on the basketball court: For years and years the four Nutt boys had city league or other teams that they called the Nutt Brothers. This actually goes back to Fordyce and Mr. Nutt and they played tons of basketball. When all four were there it was like watching the Harlem Globetrotters. All could shoot, dribble and pass. When I was in college I watched them play a city league game in Little Rock. They played at the highest level, which included high school stars, college players and former college players. Dennis was at TCU at that time. The strategy was to feed him the ball and let him do his thing. The other team was grabbing him, shoving him and even knocking him down as he was shooting and he still scored 35 points.

- The Nutt boys and I grew up in the 70s—you know the time of big hair, drugs and misbehaving. The Nutts were totally clean cut—not just in their appearance, but their life style. Mr. Nutt did not tolerate long hair, so they all kept it short and parted—a classic look when everybody else was going a little crazy. If you look at pictures from those days, there are no embarrassing afros, chops or pony tails. Don't we all wish we had listened to Mr. Nutt?

CHAPTER 12

CARRYING ON A LEGACY

FOLLOWING IN HIS FOOTSTEPS

While we were coaching and teaching, we were also raising our own family of four little boys. Houston never knew that babies were awake at night or that they needed to be fed but, when they were old enough to hold a ball in their hands, he was there.

Houston seemed to have goals set for them. At a very young age, they were throwing, catching and hitting the ball, as well as putting it through the hoop. He didn't want them to do much of anything outside of ball and they were always in training. He was adamant about three balanced meals and getting enough rest. They could only have a Coke at Fordyce when Aunt Ella took them across the highway to the store or after their games, which made Cokes a special treat!

During our sons' college days, one of the boys was home for a weekend visit. While he was talking to another brother on the phone, I overheard him say, "Did you know mom and dad have Cokes in the refrigerator?"

Houston was hard on the boys and some thought he was too hard. The boys said no—it better prepared them for coaching. Houston wanted them to devote all of their time to sports, so they could be the very best athletes they could possibly be.

ATTENDING CHURCH

To say that our lives revolved around ASD would be an understatement. When we first came to Little Rock, we attended the Antioch Missionary Baptist Church, along with some of the deaf children at ASD. It seemed to be the natural place for us to go, since Houston often times drove the bus for the children and the pastor was Houston's cousin, the late Dick Jones. Pastor Jones was a hearing man but was very fluent in sign language, because of his deaf heritage. He delivered his message with voice and signs, simultaneously. It is still done that way today at that particular church.

In the 50s, we were in the early stages of integrating our deaf students into hearing churches off campus. It was a huge step. Up to this point Sunday school was taught by teachers or houseparents on campus.

Our students were very excited to go to church "out in the world." (Any place, even a person or thing apart from the deaf-school campus was referred to as "out in the world.")

Houston and I decided our sons needed to be in a hearing church. When Houston Dale, our oldest son, was four and our second son, Dickey, was two, we visited Immanuel Baptist Church. The pastor, Dr. W. O. Vaught, was a verse-by-verse Bible teacher. He had such a strong voice and he so distinctly enunciated every word. I felt confident that Houston would love that church.

Houston agreed to visit the next Sunday but told me that we would not join that day. That was all well and good with me. After hearing Dr. Vaught that first Sunday, he was pushing me out in the aisle and to my surprise we joined that very day.

We were so fortunate to have had Dr. W. O. Vaught as our pastor and dear friend for all those years. He baptized all four of our sons and we were always thrilled when he attended the games with us at Central High! He would sit between Houston and me and I actually felt as if I were sitting next to God!

Immanuel Baptist Church, 1929 – 2003

W. O. Vaught

7301 Apache Road
Little Rock, Arkansas 72205
(501) 663-5522

May 11, 1989

Houston & Imogene Nutt
919 Bowman Road
Little Rock, AR   72211

My sweet friends,

How good it was to see you and a good many members of
your family seated there in the auditorium the Sunday I
preached at Immanuel. It was one of those days I cannot
and will not forget. Visiting your home and talking to
your boys one by one as they accepted Christ and joined
the church is a treasured memory that will never fade.

I will always count you among the very most faithful
members I had and the love I have for you and your
family abounds more and more.

Yours in friendship,

W. O. Vaught

WOV/wb

Dr. W. O. Vaught's letter to Nutt family

Nutt family at home, 311 Rice

THE BOYS' BIGGEST TREAT

Our sons actually *"cut their teeth" on basketball in that old gym. They knew time in the gym was to be treated seriously.

From the time our sons could barely dribble a basketball to the time they were seniors in high school, going to the gym was always special and it never grew old! Basketball at our house was literally rated next to our religion and some may have thought it was the other way around.

A bad attitude or behavior problem was easily solved just by mentioning the possibility of not getting to go to the gym. If things were getting **"out of hand," I could always say, "Do you want me to tell daddy?"

Even on Christmas morning, unless it was on Sunday, as soon as all the presents were opened it was the same request, "Daddy, can we go to the gym?" It seemed as if they hurriedly unwrapped every gift, getting rid of a chore so they could go to the gym. It was always a treat for them and it seemed to be treasured even more than a Christmas present!

DEAF SCHOOL ACTIVITIES WERE OUR ACTIVITIES

While the boys were growing up, they never missed Houston Sr.'s games, athletic banquets, school carnivals, the State Fair or end-of-school picnics.

When our boys were small, Fair Day was a big day every year! We'd take them out of school and they would go to the Fair with our deaf children. I think at times our boys thought *they* were even deaf and they, for sure, thought I baked more cookies for my deaf kids than I baked for them.

We went to all home games in the old gym. We also went to most of the out-of-town and even out-of-state games on the old yellow

---

* cut their teeth – learned
** out of hand - lose control

school bus. We were well aware the bus might break down somewhere along the way. We also knew our bus driver, the late Mac Windham, could fix any problem that might occur. He was a good mechanic and a great man.

The out-of-state games were with deaf schools in Oklahoma, Texas and Mississippi. We would leave on Friday and return on Sunday. We literally traveled hundreds of miles on that old yellow school bus. The boys got to pass out the sack lunches and they were so honored to do that. After giving each player a sack lunch, they would discover there were four extra lunches left and they would be so excited! That meant they could have a lunch—an apple and a bologna sandwich. They didn't know their Dad had specifically ordered four extra lunches.

When the boys reached a certain age, during games they could sit on the bench and be the towel boys. At half time, they could shoot baskets if there was no entertainment planned. Houston's players were our sons' heroes. They also learned that color or deafness didn't matter—it's the character that matters. Those valuable lessons learned in the old gym and on that old yellow school bus are now extended into a second generation as they carry on their father's legacy.

HOUSTON DALE

Our first son, Houston Dale, was born at St. Vincent Infirmary, Little Rock, Ark., on October 14, 1957 at 6:10 a.m., weighing 6 lbs., 12.5 oz.

He was given his father's name and a middle name was added to distinguish between father and son; however, I was about the only one who called him Houston Dale. He learned sign language before he could talk, as they all did. Some said that was a mistake and that he would never learn to talk. In fact, one doctor told Houston that and we never saw that doctor again.

Being the only child was short-lived. When he was 20-months-old, he had to share his parents' love with a little brother, then another and another.

Having an October birthday, Houston Dale was a seven-year-old first grader and, as you can imagine, he was more mature than most of his classmates. That was expressed to me by every teacher from kindergarten through high school, as well as the Sunday school teachers.

At age six, he was involved in organized sports—basketball, baseball and YMCA football—and was good in all. In baseball, he could hit a home run over the fence and in basketball he could dribble behind his back, between his legs, and make baskets. He was very loose—just a natural player.

Being the oldest of four boys, it was hard to get away from his little tag-a-long brothers. He would often plead, "If I could only go across the alley to play ball with my friends, I will take my little brothers and watch out for them." Sure enough, the times he got to go, he never broke that promise.

When Houston Dale was six or seven, he had this obsession about marrying me. He would say, "Mom, when I grow up, I'm going to marry you!" I explained to him again and again that little boys don't marry their moms, but he said he was going to marry me anyway. Of course he finally outgrew that stage and the focus was on pro ball. By the time he was 11 or 12 he was going to be in the NBA, NFL or both.

Along with Little League, YMCA and Boys Club games, there was the Nutt Pee Wee basketball team for the little boys. Houston Sr. organized this traveling Nutt Pee Wee team that would play every Saturday night before the big game. The Nutt Brothers, the big team, was made up of Houston Sr., his brothers, Clyde and Fay, and a few others.

After more games and practices than one could ever imagine, the Nutt Pee Wee games and Little League were left to the younger brothers, as Houston Dale advanced to junior high. For the first time, his father was not his coach. While on the junior high level, he was beginning to be noticed as an outstanding basketball and football player.

LITTLE ROCK CENTRAL HIGH

As a sophomore at Central High School, Houston Dale came out on top as varsity quarterback and led the Tigers throughout his high school career.

His caring ways extended beyond his brothers. One day he came home wagging not one, but two bags of dirty clothes from Central High football practice. He said, "Mom, can you wash these clothes for my friend, because his mother doesn't have a washing machine?" Well, of course I could do that, but as I picked up the bag I realized, from the odor, I'd have to take the whole bag outside and hose the clothes down with my head turned the other way. The clothes hadn't been washed all season and, as you can imagine, smelled really, really bad—I mean terrible! Well, I wish I could have washed his practice clothes more often. I know he appreciated having clean clothes, even if it was for one day.

Friday night high school games were big. Quigley Stadium was always packed. It was hard to find a space to park or a place to sit once inside the stadium.

Every Friday night after the game, our sons with maybe a friend or two would come home and rehash the entire game with their dad—I mean they would go over every play. A close friend even broke up with his girlfriend, temporarily, so he could be a part of this. Going over the game, play by play, seemed to be as important as playing the actual game. Houston Sr. praised the boys when they deserved it, and he also pointed out plays that didn't go so well.

Incidentally, after football season was over, our friend was back with his high school sweetheart, who later became his wife.

During Houston Dale's senior year, after the Parkview game (one of our strongest rivalries), the team came to our house for the Friday night party. The football players and some of the girlfriends came. We had the usual sandwiches, chips, cookies, popcorn, Cokes, and a bucket of Kentucky Fried Chicken that was brought by one of the players—the one who had "clean practice clothes" for a day. Our greatly loved but modest home at 311 Rice was full to the brim and fun for all!

Houston Dale had a "fairy tale" high school career. Family and relatives came from Fordyce to watch him play, especially Turkey Day games. In his senior year he led his team to a 12-0 record, winning both the conference and the state 5-A championship.

> "Houston Dale was All-State three years and All-American his junior and senior years and was considered one of the state's best quarterbacks in more than a decade. He led Central to a 30-4-1 record during his three years as quarterback. He passed for more than 3,400 yards including 1,059 yards and made 15 touchdowns in 10 games during 1975." - *Tiger Pride*, Brian Cox.

In conference action, junior Houston Nutt (left) dribbles the ball down court against Parkview

Houston Dale playing basketball for Central High Tigers

Houston Dale as Central High quarterback

COACH BEAR BRYANT'S VISIT

He had many scholarship offers, including one from Coach Bear Bryant of Alabama. How exciting that was!

Everyone has heard about Coach Bryant wrestling a bear in Fordyce but we have our own Coach "Bear" Bryant stories. He played football for the Fordyce *Redbugs*, the only high school in America to claim that name for its mascot.

When Houston Dale was a senior in high school, Coach "Bear" Bryant paid us a visit at 311 Rice Street. We tried to keep it quiet but word had gotten around. There were many cars parked near our house, trying to get a glimpse of Paul "Bear" Bryant or at least his hounds-tooth hat. I didn't blame them.

Our four sons were playing basketball in the back yard when Coach Bryant and his cousin, Mr. Kilgore, arrived. The ball had gone over the big wooden gates and the coach threw the ball in. He told the boys to continue the game, but that was hard to do with Coach Bryant watching.

We went inside and gathered around Coach Bryant. "After having watched you boys play," he said, "I'll take all four boys. Now, you need to think about this offer. The other three boys, as good as they are, may not be as widely recruited as Houston Dale but this way all their college education will be paid. I can tell they'll earn a scholarship at Alabama in basketball or football."

After a while, Coach Bryant shifted from the Crimson Tide to telling stories about growing up near Fordyce on the Cotton Belt. He told us how he stayed home from school at times to help his mother. They would load the peas and buttermilk in the wagon and go to town, which was Fordyce. They had to go by the school on the way to the Kilgore Store. Some of the boys would make fun of him as he passed the school in the wagon, and he said, "I know who they are today."

His mother would have lunch with her family, but he said, "As a young boy, I'd take my cheese and crackers and climb on top of the train to eat." You could feel the love and respect he had for his mother as he told of her integrity and work ethic. He clearly credited his mother for his success.

Houston Dale's visit to Alabama was different from all the others because of the early signing period. Coach Bryant took Houston Dale into his home and made him feel very special. He entertained him for the most part and he will always remember that special time and conversation with Coach "Bear" Bryant. "You play for me—you'll be a millionaire," he said, mentioning Joe Namath as well as others.

Mary Harmon, his wife, would say, "You won't get homesick, we won't let you." Close to the signing date she called often, assuring us of Houston Dale's good care. It was a very hard decision—with people talking to him, the phone ringing off the wall, and letters that filled three garbage bags. He had to make a decision between Arkansas and Alabama.

Coach Broyles' words were weighing heavy, "The University of Arkansas is home and you can throw a rock from your house to the stadium." After much debate, on the last signing day he chose the University of Arkansas.

The press conference to announce the signing was at our home. Among the distinguished guests were: Coach Frank Broyles; Coach Eddie Sutton; Cathey and Ken Turner; Dave Woodman, our Immanuel friend with Channel 4; and our pastor, Dr. W. O. Vaught, who was dressed in his red Razorback blazer.

UNIVERSITY OF ARKANSAS – FOOTBALL AND BASKETBALL

Transitioning from high school to college is a big step, especially in the football arena. As a true freshman, it's not always a good situation to be a starting quarterback, but that's exactly what happened to Houston Dale. The starting quarterback was injured and he was the starting quarterback for four games.

When football season was over, he played basketball for Eddie Sutton and lettered in 1976-77. During that time, they played a tournament in Brazil and won the whole thing, including the Governor's Cup.

While in Brazil, the players bought vases for their mothers that were made from large, brown-glass jugs. Houston Dale held that vase in his hands on the 28-hour flight home. During that trip, Coach Sutton commented, "I hope your mother appreciates that vase." The other players packed their vases in their bags and their moms never got them because they were broken into a zillion pieces. While preparing for the move from 311 Rice, the boys were helping us pack and discard different things. They would say, "Toss this, toss that," and when they came to the Brazilian vase, someone said, "Toss it!" Houston Dale stopped what he was doing and looked at me, as I looked at him, shaking his head, he said, "They don't understand!" No, they did not understand! That vase was not tossed and has a special place on the top shelf in Houston Sr.'s office. And yes, I do appreciate the vase.

After the 1976 football season, something happened that we would have never dreamed. Coach Frank Broyles stepped down. It was absolutely devastating! Coach Broyles recruited Houston Dale with the promise of all the great things he would likely achieve. You can imagine the disappointment.

Lou Holtz replaced Coach Broyles, and he ran an option-oriented offense. Since Houston Dale was a drop-back passer and the fact Coach Holtz brought a quarterback with him, he was not certain what his future would be.

Houston Dale was a native Arkansan with very favorable press during his junior high and high school years and fans were constantly nagging Lou Holtz to play him more. As you can imagine, this formed a strained relationship.

One day Coach Holtz called Houston Dale to his office. Pointing to a stack of letters, he said, "Look, it's only Tuesday and I've received 50 letters and 100 phone calls about your playing time." Houston Dale felt like he was causing a problem, and that maybe he should get out of the way.

Houston Dale with family, Coach Eddie Sutton and
Frank Broyles, signing to play for Razorbacks

Arkansas Razorbacks football

Congratulations 1977 Basketball Razorbacks from one First team to another.

Basketball Razorbacks

Houston Dale in action for OSU

OKLAHOMA STATE

After the Orange Bowl in 1978, a final decision was made to transfer to Oklahoma State.

Coach Stanley, the Oklahoma State coach, who highly recruited Houston Dale in high school, was honored to have him, even though it was two years *"down the road." The transfer was **"out of the frying pan into the fire!" Coach Stanley was fired before Houston Dale became eligible to play. It couldn't have gotten any worse than that! Coach Jimmy Johnson replaced Coach Stanley and Coach Leahy was his new quarterback coach. He yelled, screamed and cursed. It was a harrowing experience! Day after day, he endured the haranguing. It was unbelievable! He finally worked into playing time as quarterback—basketball, too, for that matter!

After the last week of football during Houston Dale's senior year, a shocking thing happened. Coach Leahy came to his room and asked his friends to please leave the room. The coach closed the door and told Houston Dale to sit down on the bed. He had no idea what was going to take place. The coach started off by saying he just wanted to let him know he had changed his life, and then he said, "In spite of the way I treated you, every day you came to practice with a smile on your face. You had something I wanted and it's because of you that I am now a Christian!" Well, as you can imagine, thoughts were twirling in Houston Dale's head. He was astounded and speechless! Never in a lifetime would he have dreamed something like that! WOW!

When asked about the transfer to OSU, Houston Dale said, "If I had it to do over I would NOT transfer! It's a very tough deal, but on the other hand, had I not transferred I would not have had the opportunity to meet some people who have been a great influence in my life. And a soul may not have been saved!"

---

* down the road - a later time
** out of the frying pan into the fire - from a bad situation into one that is worse

GRAD ASSISTANT

After graduation in 1981, Jimmy Johnson said, "Houston, you are my graduate assistant." He didn't realize at the time what a wonderful opportunity that was and that's when his coaching career began. In 1983 he returned to Arkansas as a graduate assistant under Lou Holtz. This time the relationship was not a strained one; instead, it was a very good one.

Houston Dale said he attributes his success to the coaches he has had in his life, beginning with mom and dad, Coach Ripley, Joe Fred Young, Bernie Cox, Clyde Horton, Eddie Boone, Johnny Greenwood, Coach Broyles, Lou Holtz, Eddie Sutton, Pat Foster, Gene Keady, Pat Jones, Paul Hansen, Jim Killingsworth, and Jimmy Johnson.

ASSISTANT COACH

Houston Dale's first full-time position came at Arkansas State in the spring of 1984 under Larry Lacewell. Before the season got under way, he got an offer to return to OSU. He was under Pat Jones at OSU for six seasons as the Cowboys Receivers Coach. Heisman trophy winner, Barry Sanders, All-Americans Thurman Thomas and Hart Lee Dykes all played for the OSU Cowboys during his tenure.

In 1990 Houston Dale returned to the University of Arkansas as the Razorbacks Receivers Coach for two years under head coach Jack Crowe.

HEAD COACH/MURRAY STATE

Houston Dale's first head-coaching job was at Murray State University in Murray, Kentucky, in 1992. The Racers won back-to-back championships. In 1995, he was named Ohio Valley Conference Coach of the Year and Sports Network/Eddie Robinson National Division 1-AA Coach of the Year. In 1996, he was named Ohio Valley Conference and Regional Coach of the Year.

BOISE STATE

His first Division I job was at Boise State, in Boise, Idaho, where the games were played on blue turf. After a successful year, suddenly he was in the running for the head-coaching job at the University of Arkansas.

UNIVERSITY OF ARKANSAS

Houston Dale was introduced as the 29th head football coach of the University of Arkansas on December 10, 1997. It was indeed his dream job! He said during the press conference, "I will work from sunup to exhaustion." (His two grandfathers would have been so proud had they heard that.)

Frank Broyles said, "I've never seen fans respond to a coach like our fans have to Houston. They believed in him before he ever coached a game here. Houston's enthusiasm is so overwhelming that we were able to expand our stadium to 72,000 seats." Coach Nutt already finds himself in the elite company in the school record books. He is only the third head coach in U. of A. history to lead the Hogs to bowl games in each of his first six seasons. The other two coaches who accomplished this were Lou Holtz and Ken Hatfield.

In his first year at Arkansas, the Razorbacks were picked to finish last in the SEC West, but he won the first eight games. They finished 9-3 and won a share of the SEC Western Division title and made their first trip to the Florida Citrus Bowl. They concluded the season in the top 20, and Coach Nutt was named the Football News' National Coach of the Year.

In his second year, the Hogs became the Western Division favorite because of an unusually large senior class. Although they had trouble on the road, they finished in the manner of legends, defeating No. 3 Tennessee and No. 12 Mississippi on consecutive weekends to earn a spot in the Cotton Bowl. They played their long-time rival, Texas. The well-prepared team handed the Longhorns a 27-6 loss in front of a packed stadium. For the first time in school history, Texas was held to negative rushing yards. Once again, the Hogs finished in the top 20 and, I might add, that was the first bowl victory in 15 years.

The third year, in the fall of 2000, he faced his toughest challenge yet without Clint Stoerner, one of the best passers in the history of the school, and receiver Anthony Lucas. This was a year of injuries. Nine players were lost for the season to injury, including the top three tailbacks. Despite all the injuries, he rallied his team to back-to-back wins over No. 13 Mississippi State and No. 24 LSU to secure yet another winning regular season and a bowl game—the Las Vegas Bowl, which was played in December, 2000.

In 2001, the Razorbacks stumbled to a 1-3 start including three straight losses in league play. The coach and the Hogs rebounded to win six of their final seven regular-season games. The Razorbacks topped No. 9 South Carolina 10-7 and No. 17 Auburn 42-17.

The Hogs fought their way back to Dallas for a New Year's Day game, with the defending national champion, Oklahoma, in the Cotton Bowl. I have never been as cold as I was on that day January 1, 2002. Unfortunately, the Hogs lost 10-3.

The 2002 season started impressively with convincing wins over Boise State and South Florida. After losing at home to Alabama and a road defeat at Tennessee in six overtimes, the Razorbacks hope for a division title looked bleak! Once again, Houston Dale rallied his team in winning five straight games, including road conference wins at South Carolina and Mississippi State. This gave the Hogs a chance for a share of the SEC Western Division crown.

Trailing nationally ranked LSU with less than a minute to play, quarterback Matt Jones found De Cori Birmingham in the back of the end zone for a 31-yard touchdown pass. This gave the Hogs a share of the SEC Western Division title and the opportunity to play in the SEC Championship game in Atlanta, Georgia. Arkansas made its second appearance in the league championship game and ended the season at the Music City Bowl.

The Razorbacks wasted no time getting noticed in 2003, defeating No. 5 Texas, 38-28 in a nationally televised game at Austin. Arkansas vaulted into the national polls to No. 14, marking the highest debut of any team since the poll was expanded to 25 teams in 1989. Arkansas rallied for a 34-31 double-overtime win at Alabama to keep the momentum going. After three heartbreaking conference losses, the Hogs salvaged its season with a historic 71-63 seven-overtime win at Kentucky. They tied their own record of a seven-overtime period set in 2001 and played two of the longest games in NCAA history.

The Razorbacks went on to win four of the last five games, including their Independence Bowl game against Missouri 27-14. After winning the Independence Bowl in late December 2003, there was no time to enjoy it.

The word was that Nebraska was pursuing Houston Dale. They first offered him $2 million then raised it to $2.5 million. It would have been so easy to walk away, with the onset of the investigation and probation relating to irregularities, before he was hired and how it was going to affect the next two years. The NCAA penalties were going to reduce Arkansas' recruiting classes by a total of seven players over three years. The program's overall scholarship limit of 85 would be cut to 83 since the 2001-2002 academic year and would remain capped through 2005-2006.

The Nebraska plane was parked on the tarmac waiting to whisk Houston Dale away. He said he was on his knees all night, searching for the right decision and contemplating the spoken words from Dad, whose advice was highly respected. He felt a resounding "STAY HOME!" and, when the time came, he felt he could not get on that plane and take his family to Nebraska.

Coach Broyles opened a morning news conference by saying: "This is a day of celebration that Houston is going to remain as our football coach and let me just say that he is the best man for the job anywhere in America."

He endured two losing seasons 2004 and 2005 due to the NCAA penalties due from the previous staff. Coach Broyles assured him of his support through the difficult years. Houston Dale said it was the toughest two years he'd ever been through.

The next year, with a clean slate and all restrictions lifted, the Hogs finished 10-2 and won the SEC West title outright! The Razorbacks were on their way to play the Florida Gators in the title game! Florida took advantage of blocked and fumbled punts to score two touchdowns in a 38-28 victory in the Georgia Dome. Now the Hogs had a No. 12 national ranking and 10-3 record going into the January 1 Capitol One Bowl against 11-1 Wisconsin in Orlando, Fla. Unfortunately, Darren McFadden hurt his shoulder on the first play, but Felix Jones, a sophomore from Tulsa, Okla., stepped up and scored two touchdowns but the Razorbacks lost to Wisconsin 17-14.

Finishing the 2006 year 10-4, 7-1 SEC record and in the top 20, Coach Broyles said, "We're celebrating the 2006 season and we're still building for next year with hopes of being improved. That's all I'm concentrating on."

In Houston Dale's tenure at Arkansas, the Hogs played in the 1999 Citrus Bowl, 2000 Cotton Bowl, 2000 Las Vegas Bowl, 2002 Cotton Bowl, 2002 Music Bowl and 2003 Independence Bowl, 2006 Citrus Bowl, and the 2007 Cotton Bowl. In November 2007 he was hired by Ole Miss and didn't get to coach his team for that last bowl game.

His 10-year reign in his dream job at the University of Arkansas ended just three days after one of the greatest victories of his coaching career, a 50-48 triple-overtime victory at No. 1 LSU on Friday, November 23, 2007. He passed Lou Holtz for most wins only behind Frank Broyles.

His tenure is the third longest among Arkansas coaches behind outgoing Athletic Director Frank Broyles' 19 seasons from 1958-1976 and Fred Thomsen's 13 seasons from 1929-1941. *Author's note: Statistics taken from University of Arkansas Media Guide.*

OLE MISS

Houston Dale was introduced as Mississippi's 36th football coach on Wednesday, November 28, 2007. He, his wife Diana, and their daughter, Haven, were introduced to a standing-ovation crowd at the Ford Center for Performing Arts in Oxford, Miss. There couldn't have been a better beginning! They won back-to-back Cotton Bowl victories for the first time since 1960-61.

In 2009, they defeated No. 8 Texas Tech 47-34; defeated No. 18 Oklahoma State, 21-7. Then after two losing seasons he was dismissed.

Houston and Frank Broyles

THE TOP 25 SINGLE-GAME ATTENDANCE MARKS IN SCHOOL HISTORY HAVE ALL COME SINCE HOUSTON NUTT BECAME HEAD COACH.

WITH SEVEN BOWL BIDS IN THE LAST NINE YEARS, ARKANSAS IS TIED FOR THE LEAD IN THE SEC'S WESTERN DIVISION.

IN HIS NINE YEARS AS HEAD COACH, THE HOGS HAVE EARNED ALL-SEC RECOGNITION 52 TIMES AND SEC ACADEMIC HONOR ROLL HONORS 145 TIMES.

Houston Dale – University of Arkansas Head Coach

Murray State Coach Houston Nutt (in straw hat) is enjoying success with his Arkansas Connection. Assistants
from Arkansas include Kim Damron (back middle), Danny Nutt (front right), and Mark Hutson (behind Danny
Nutt). Players include (back row, from left) Mike Cherry
(18), Ramon Okoli, Reuel Shepherd (14), Tim Scarbor-
ough (22) and Ronnie Merritt, (middle row) Elliott Dunn
(24), Tony Turner, Shawn McDermott and William
Hampton (31), Ray Hoover (seated in truck bed), and
Reginald Swinton (front).

Houston Dale - Murray State Head Coach

Head coach Houston
Nutt led the Rebels to
back-to-back nine-win
seasons for the first
time since 1961-62.

OLE MISS SUCCESS
UNDER HOUSTON NUTT

Houston Dale – Ole Miss Head Coach

Houston Dale is married to the former Diana Lynn Thomas of Oklahoma City and a graduate of OSU. They have four children: Houston III, twins Hanna and Hailey, and Haven. He is currently an analyst for CBS Sports Network and Sirius XM Radio.

Houston Dale's family

DICKEY

Our second son, Dickey, was born on June 13, 1959, at high noon. He missed being that "eight-pound, bouncing baby boy" by only three ounces. Being the second son, he was given my maiden name, Dickey. He had beautiful auburn hair and a personality that seemed to radiate playful mischief, so you see why he was always the center of attention. Everywhere we went people would stop us to comment on Dickey's hair and the other boys couldn't understand why people didn't comment on their hair. One day after an outing, Houston Dale came to me with a very solemn face and said, "Momma, is my hair pretty too?" I said, "Yes, why do you ask?" He said, "Everyone always says Dickey's hair is pretty!"

All of the boys attended Our Lady of Holy Souls, the Catholic school on Center Street. Houston Dale and Dickey completed grades one through three, while Danny and Dennis were in kindergarten and nursery. Although the German Sisters spoke very little English, they more than made up for it with their kindness and goodness. It was well worth the drive across town.

When Dickey was about two or three-years old, he insisted on saying the blessing at home as the Sisters did at school. He would go through the whole ritual, by touching his forehead and each side of his chest, while saying, "In the name of the Father, Son, and Holy Toast." We never convinced him it was, "Holy Ghost." The Sisters eventually returned to Germany and the school closed.

I don't know if it was Dickey's auburn hair or his out-going personality, but everyone was drawn to him, especially his uncle Fred who picked at him unmercifully. He would bypass the other boys looking for Dickey so he could pester him. He would tease, pick at him and sometimes even make him mad, just to hear his quick retort. He called him all kinds of names, even a "billy goat," to *"get a rise out of" him, and when he got the response he was expecting, he would laugh until his stomach literally bobbed up and down.

One day while Dickey was visiting his grandma, he was watching TV and Fred came in. Dickey was prepared for him. He pretended to be very involved in the cartoons he was watching. He knew Fred was standing there, trying to think of some way to pester him. Without taking his eyes off the screen, Dickey reached over, took a tissue from the box and stuffed it into his mouth and started chewing it. Since he knew Fred was going to call him a goat, he thought he would **"beat him to the draw." Fred burst out with laughter, slapping his legs, pointing at Dickey, saying, "I told you! I told you! " By this time every one was in the living room to see what all the commotion was about and we all had a big laugh! Dickey was not disappointed with his uncle's reaction.

Having an older brother, Dickey always had someone to play with and that was ideal. After a few years, he joined his brother, Houston Dale, on the YMCA football team, the Boys Club basketball team, as well as the Nutt Pee Wee team. He also played Little League and Pony League baseball, coached by his dad.

Dickey enjoyed all three sports but basketball was his favorite. There was always a basketball game going on either in the back yard or at the gym. Basketball was year-round. The boys could walk to the deaf school since there was a catwalk over Markham Street, and we didn't worry about them crossing the street.

After many wonderful years and more games than anyone could possibly imagine, it was time for junior high. Dickey played basketball and football in junior high and experienced for the first time a coach other than his dad. In addition to football and basketball, he worked the lunch line taking up lunch money, as most of our sons did, and considered it an honor. One of the perks was that they could have two lunches, extra rolls, cookies and milk—whatever they wanted.

---

* get a rise out of - a response
** beat to the draw – to be the first to say or do something

However, Dickey experienced one incident he probably had rather forget. One of the students in the lunch line kept saying, *"let me slide." The conversation continued getting a little more heated as the student got closer to the cash register. Dickey refused to give him a free lunch ticket and the boy picked up a chair and hit him over the head. The fight was on and both boys were expelled from school.

They were supposed to go to a "special" school across town for a certain number of days. Houston Sr. refused to send Dickey to that school because he thought it had a bad reputation, so we kept Dickey at home. After his head wound healed, he returned to school, resumed his job taking up lunch tickets, and everything was good after that.

Dickey, #15, quarterback for YMCA football team

---

* let me slide - get something free

Boys Club basketball -Dickey #27 and Danny #15, Houston Sr., coach

LITTLE ROCK CENTRAL HIGH

During Dickey's sophomore and junior years at Central High, he was backup quarterback for Houston Dale and he would send in the plays using sign language. As the story goes, on one occasion we were ahead, so instead of sending in the play, Dickey signed, "Hey, we're ahead 20 points, come out, I want to play!"

Following an undefeated state championship, his team had only two returning lettermen on offense and their work was *"cut out" for them. Being one year behind Houston Dale meant he had only one year to quarterback the team, but first he would have to earn that right. It was game by game, but by mid-season Dickey led the Tigers to a victory over the NLR Ole Main Wildcats, which locked in the starting quarterback position for the rest of the season.

---

* cut out – must face a large task

ANNUAL THANKSGIVING GAME

We were all gearing up for the annual Thanksgiving Day game with Hall High School at Quigley Stadium. That was a big day! It was Dickey's turn to be quarterback and the stands would be packed with eight to twelve thousand fans. I had been cooking for a week and the relatives from Fordyce were coming to watch Dickey play. As to how we enjoyed the Thanksgiving dinner, of course, depended on the outcome of the game.

The Tigers led 10-3 in the fourth quarter. After the ball was punted to the Hall 20, it bounced toward the original line of scrimmage. As the ball was rolling past the 39, it was touched and the official threw his hat down on the ground. Our boys assumed it was the end of play but the official's action did not end the play. The opponent picked up the ball and ran approximately 50 yards for a touchdown. After a two-point conversion, the score was 11-10 in their favor. I still feel the numbness. We were all in shock! That was a devastating loss because we thought we had the game won. Dickey had played a near perfect game and we felt like we had been robbed. We did the best we could with the turkey, dressing and all the trimmings on that Thanksgiving Day. After this game, Dickey was especially happy to join the basketball team. He was in his element.

Central High was and still is a very special high school. Dickey not only was voted by his classmates the most popular boy in his senior class, but he made life-long friends. At least one of those friends is his very best friend today.

Central finished the season in a tie for third place in conference. Dickey was a three-year letterman on championship football and basketball teams during his high school career.

Dickey, #1, quarterback for Central High Tigers football team

Dickey in action on Central High Tigers basketball team

COLLEGE CAREER

Although Dickey enjoyed football in high school, he wanted to play only basketball in college. Turning down scholarship offers from smaller schools, fortunately he got a scholarship at OSU playing at his parents' alma mater. He had the good fortune of playing for great coaches like the late Jim Killingsworth and the late Paul Hansen. Coach Hansen would often talk about Dickey being, "one of the best, if not the best shooter on the team, and deadly from 20 feet." Nothing pleased Dad more than that!

During Dickey's second year at OSU, Houston Dale, who had transferred from Arkansas, joined him. They lived in the same dorm and played on the same basketball team, which was wonderful! This was like old times, playing on the same team as they did in their younger years and in high school.

The boys had a wonderful host family at OSU, Bob and Sally Arhberg. They often had the boys in their home and prepared wonderful meals, especially during holidays. They made them feel so at home while away from home. We could never repay them.

Dickey at OSU

Dickey in action at OSU

STUDENT TEACHING

During Dickey's practice teaching at Stillwater High School, he had no idea how important sign-language skills would be. A student was having a particularly hard time in life and it was as if an angel had dropped from heaven to help that person. And that angel was Dickey, who just happened to have sign language skills.

This student was having so many problems that he was on the verge of being expelled from school, but that was not the worst part.

He was so distressed that he had drawn a picture of a grave and pointed to himself. He was miserable and wanted to die.

He was the only deaf student at the school. There was no one who could communicate fluently with him at home or school. There was an interpreter but he either didn't understand or chose not to obey. The student's family was from Taiwan and their language was Taiwanese. They worked out-of-state most of the time and his grandmother stayed home with him. He communicated with gestures or a few homemade signs and he was so troubled, sad and lonely.

Dickey goes into this school and meets this young man who is deaf. Naturally, Dickey begins talking to him and I can almost see his face light up! He was so happy to have someone that could talk to him. On the first day of practice teaching, the young man did everything he was told to do—he even dressed out in his P.E. clothes. Dickey did not know he had refused to dress out for the whole year. The teachers and others on campus all gathered around and wanted to know how Dickey convinced him to change clothes. There was nothing to it, Dickey told him to change and he did. While Dickey was there, this student participated in all of his classes, interacting with his classmates and teachers for the first time. This student loved Dickey and clung to him like a magnet. If Dickey had told him to *"jump into the fire," I'm sure he would have done it!

The young man's grandmother told Dickey that he had saved her grandson's life. He was so happy for nine weeks and everyone thought he was **"on the right track." But when Dickey's practice teaching was over, the student immediately returned to his pattern of bad behavior. At first, he was having trouble in the lunchroom, so Dickey arranged to go to the school every day for lunch. Then, there were problems in P. E. and Dickey went back for P. E. Each day they added another class, so finally Dickey worked it out, so he could go to school with the student all day. With Dickey's help, he graduated that spring!

Angels are real—ask this young man!

---

* jump into the fire - totally trust
** on the right track – priorities in order

"A child who is a member of a linguistic minority, as well as being deaf, will start to live in three culturally different worlds: at home, in school and with peers. Each has its own mode of communication which requires the deaf child to become tri-lingual/tri-cultural using the family's native language in the home, English at school and signing with deaf peers.

"Deaf children from non-English families are three to four times more likely to be labeled learning disabled, mentally retarded or emotionally disturbed." - Dr. Robert K. Rittenhouse, *Deaf Education at the Dawn of the 21st Century,* p. 64.

DEGREES

Dickey received his Bachelor of Science degree in physical education in 1982 and his master's degree in athletic administration from OSU in 1984. (In my opinion, he should have an honorary degree in deaf psychology.)

FIRST JOB: ASSISTANT COACH

Dickey's first assistant coaching job came in 1983-85 at Stillwater High School in Stillwater, Okla. In 1985-87 he was part-time assistant at Oklahoma State.

In 1987-95 Dickey was the assistant men's basketball coach at Arkansas State in Jonesboro, Ark., located in the northeast corner of the state. All of Dickey's children were born there, and they lived there over twenty-two years.

HEAD COACHING JOB

Dickey got an opportunity to be interim coach at ASU in 1995. The athletic director was Dr. Brad Hovious, who is currently associate athletic director at Rice University.

Dickey was promoted under unusual circumstances. Because of budget restraints and the firing of the head coach, he would make the same salary as he made as an assistant which was $31,355 yearly. There were many stipulations: rebuild the ASU recruiting base, mend fences with high school and AAU coaches, improve ticket sales and attendance, bring enthusiasm back into the game and –win! In spite of these unusual circumstances he was delighted to accept the head-coaching job; in fact, he probably would have done it for nothing.

During his time, the ASU Convocation Center was referred to as the "Nutt House," and peanuts were tossed in the stands during those exciting games!

In his third year they won the Sun Belt Conference with a record of 20-9 and he was named Coach of the Year. In his fourth year, they went to the Conference Tournament and won it all, taking his team to the NCAA tournament, which had never been done in the history of the school nor has it been done since.

As you see, the requirements were met and Dickey was a full-fledged head coach. He was the head coach at ASU from 1995-2008.

THE NCAA TOURNAMENT

It is every coach's ambition to take his team to the NCAA tournament, and to accomplish this is remarkable!

The year Dickey took his team to New Orleans for the NCAA tournament, his brother, Dennis, was on his staff and had a part in this NCAA experience as well. Also attending the games were the coaches' families, Mom, Dad, older brother, Houston Dale and ASU's faithful fans. It was a very exciting experience!

The Arkansas State University Media Guide gave this account:

> "The first half was close, with the Indians actually leading, 15-14 with 8:32 to play when Utah began to muscle into the lead. Tony Harvey nailed a three with 25 seconds to go, giving the Utes a half-time lead of 36-30.

"Freddie Hicks loomed large inside and swatted away four shots in the half. Chico Fletcher scored 15 points to keep the score close. Down one (39-38) with 16:22 left, ASU began to succumb to the size disadvantage inside. The Utes established dominance and pushed the lead to 21 over the next 3:47 and kept the lead for the rest of the game.

"Hicks, ASU's all-time shot blocker, ended the game with six blocks—the third-most in NCAA Midwest Regional history. Fletcher scored 21 for the game and Beatty added 17."

Even though they lost the game, it was a remarkable accomplishment. The 1999 team was a very special team and is recorded in the history books at ASU as a NCAA tournament participant.

DAD'S QUESTION

When the boys were coaching, whether it was basketball or football, they always knew where their dad sat and they talked to him by using sign language. They always thought that was pretty cool until, in one game, Houston Sr. got Dickey's attention and asked, "Why is number 25 not in the game?" This story about Dickey and his dad has been told at various gatherings, even at Houston Sr.'s funeral.

COACH OF THE YEAR

Dickey was named Sun Belt Conference Coach of the Year in 1997-1998, and received National Association of Basketball Coaches honors as District 9 Coach of the Year - 1997-98 and 1998-99. He and his staff own three Sun Belt Championship rings and rank second in the Sun Belt for all-time career conference victories.

A MOTIVATIONAL SPEAKER

During one of his motivational talks, Dickey said, "If I had told you 13 years ago that I would become the head coach at ASU and win three championships and become the second winningest coach in the Sun Belt Conference—two games shy of being the winningest coach in Arkansas State basketball history behind Gene Bartow—or that I would take my team to the NCAA tournament—which had never been done in the history of the school—you would have laughed me out of this building. Don't be afraid to dream! Dreams come true!"

A BIG GAME

During Dickey's coaching career, one of the highlights was when Eddie Sutton brought his Oklahoma State Cowboys to Jonesboro. The Convocation Center was filled to near capacity. Dickey tells the story like this:

> "It was a huge game! Mom and Dad came to the house before the game like they did for most games. My dad had a way of saying most anything in order to build our confidence to the highest level. With Eddie Sutton in town, my dad could sense I was nervous.
>
> "As I was leaving the house, my dad stopped me. I thought he was going to give me some last minute advice for the game, instead he said, 'When you walk out on that floor tonight, just know that you are five of Eddie Sutton.' I thought, *'Oh, No, Eddie Sutton is a GIANT in the world of basketball, a Hall of Famer, and a legend. Besides all that, he's someone our whole family loves very much.'*
>
> "As I was driving off, I saw my dad's hand with five fingers stretched rigidly in the air.

"Once inside the gym, I walked to mid-court to greet Coach Sutton. After a few words we wished each other good luck and returned to our opposite benches.

"Standing there, watching Coach Sutton, dad's indelible words, "You're five of Eddie Sutton" and those five fingers came to mind. Of course, that's my dad's motivational talk and it worked! I know I'm not five of Eddie Sutton, but it put me at ease."

Oklahoma State missed three-point opportunities to tie the game in the final minute and ASU held them to 36 percent shooting from the field. What a game! Arkansas State defeated Oklahoma State, 53-51. How excited we were! We couldn't believe it!

What did Eddie Sutton have to say about the loss? "You never like to lose, but if you have to lose, you like to lose to people you like."

Yes, he is a giant!

*Dickey's ASU Indians playing Eddie Sutton's
Oklahoma Cowboys in Jonesboro, AR*

1999 Sunbelt Conference Champions

Dickey at ASU

ASU Head Coach Dickey Nutt with brother, Dennis

AN UNFORGETTABLE BIRTHDAY

Dickey will never forget his 42nd birthday, when he actually experienced - *"It is more blessed to give than to receive"* (Acts 20:35, NKJV).

Not only was Dickey the basketball coach at ASU, but he had an active role in the community, as well. When the Parker Park Community Center was being built for the underprivileged children in north Jonesboro, there were not enough funds to complete it. Dickey and Cathy pledged $43,875, approximately half the cost for the two basketball courts for the facility, and these funds were matched by the city.

This allowed the Parker Park Community Center to complete the only regulation-size basketball courts available to the public in Jonesboro and it bears the name, "The Dickey Nutt Gymnasium." Having grown up in the deaf school gymnasium, Dickey and his brothers know first-hand the value of youth sports in children's lives.

On this special night the Center was brimming full. The Jennings Osborne family served approximately 1,500 heaping trays of turkey legs, ribs, BBQ sandwiches, sausages, beans, slaw, etc. People who have eaten with the Osbornes know there was enough food on those trays to last a week!

The crowd included some of Arkansas' most notable sports celebrities: Arkansas head basketball coach Nolan Richardson; Arkansas football coach Houston Nutt; ASU football coach Joe Hollis; former Pro-bowl tight end and Little Rock native, Keith Jackson; and former ASU football coach, now the Dallas Cowboys Scouting Director, Coach Larry Lacewell.

Keith Jackson, who built a similar facility in Little Rock, told the audience that it was the community that could make a difference in children's lives.

Larry Lacewell may have said it best: "The Nutts are giving great opportunities to those who really don't have a lot of opportunities in life."

"Celebrities Celebrating Children," was indeed a very special event and they're giving a gift that will keep on giving to underprivileged children truly says, *"It is more blessed to give than receive."* (Acts 20:35 – NIV).

Dickey visiting with Mitzi and Jennings Osborne as they serve the crowd their famous barbeque

RESIGNATION

On February 19, 2008, Dickey resigned with only three games left to finish his 13th season as head coach and three victories shy of being the all-time winningest coach in Arkansas State basketball history. The resignation was not of his volition, of course.

Ironically, with Dickey's departure, came the demise of their beloved mascot, the "Indians." Dickey was head coach at ASU for 13 seasons and made history that has not been repeated up to this time.

SECOND HEAD COACHING JOB

In 2009, Dickey became the 19th head basketball coach at Southeast Missouri State, better known as SEMO, at Cape Girardeau, Mo.

The university sits on the highest hill overlooking Mark Twain's Mississippi River. Dickey accepted this job at an all-time low and was hoping to take it to the next level. During the season, 2011-2012, he had the rare privilege of coaching his two sons, Logan and Luke.

Improvement has been made each year. The 2012-13-basketball season ended in tournament play and 17 wins and the 2013-14 season ended with tournament play and 18 wins.

Dickey achieved a milestone this year in his coaching when he reached his 250th win in Division I basketball. The thing that made it most significant was the fact that his son, Luke, who plays for him, broke SEMO State's record for having the most assists in the history of the school.

Dickey as head coach at SEMO State

Dickey is married to the former Cathy Thompson, a graduate of OSU. They have three children, Logan, Luke, and Lexis, who also reside in Missouri.

Dickey's family

DANNY

It was springtime in Little Rock, Ark. on May 7, 1961 when a third son was born. He kept us up all night, arriving at 3:38 a.m. and was just a beautiful baby with dark hair and olive skin. We named him Danny Alan.

Houston Dale was three-and-a-half and Dickey lacked one month being two and they seemed very happy about the addition of a baby brother. They came in often from play to check on him, as if they expected him to go out and play.

By the time Danny was about three—maybe four, he was dressed in a baseball uniform and was the batboy for his older brothers' team. He learned from them that ball was just about the most important thing in the world. When he was five or six, he was signed up and ready to play whatever sport was in season—Little League baseball, YMCA football and much, much basketball. He knew well how things were done in each sport. He did well in all three—just like his two older brothers.

The boys spent a lot of time on the baseball and football fields and at the deaf school gym. If they were not at one of those places, you could always find them in the backyard involved in a very important game.

Little League baseball: Batboys Danny (on bottom row right) and brother, Dennis, next to him. Dickey is shown third from left in middle row. Coach Nutt and Houston Dale (top row 4th and 5th from left);

YMCA football: Dickey, asst. coach, and Houston Sr., coach, on back row. Danny shown at second from left on front row.

When Danny was about eight years old, a special family moved to Little Rock from Mississippi. The father checked around to get advice concerning Little League ball for his son and he said with each inquiry he came up with the same name, Houston Nutt. Even though the roster was full, Houston Sr. became Roger's basketball, football and baseball coach for that year and throughout his Little League years. Roger and Danny became best friends and they were either at Roger's house or he was at our house.

There were many practices and games in football, baseball, and basketball, and there was a traveling Pee Wee basketball team as well. We traveled to destinations all over the state of Arkansas.

In the midst of our happy-go-lucky, carefree world something happened that changed our lives forever—Roger's mother passed away. Up to this time, our sons had not experienced the loss of a relative or dear friend. It was spring break and Danny and Dennis were in the back yard playing basketball. I called them in and explained it to them. It was as if life—the very sustenance—was drained from their bodies. I will never forget how they both sat down on the couch, side by side, without moving or saying a word, and just stared straight ahead for a long, long time. It was devastating to them, as it was for the rest of us, as well.

It seemed from that day forward our whole family adopted Roger. He fit right in, even though his blonde hair didn't match. Those outside our family thought he belonged to us, because he was with us so much and we gladly claimed him. They referred to him as "your son with blonde hair." I lost my mother at age seven and I saw my whole life flash before me. Needless to say, Roger could have gotten away with most anything.

Danny continued playing football and basketball in junior high, although he had a coach other than his dad for the first time.

LITTLE ROCK CENTRAL HIGH

It seemed that overnight Danny was at Central High. He was the third Nutt brother to be quarterback for the Tigers football team and play point guard on the basketball team. Like his oldest brother, he earned the quarterback position as a sophomore and led the Tigers throughout his high school career. It was during the second half of the West Memphis game that he became the starting quarterback. He scored on a one-yard run and completed a 21-yard touchdown pass to Teddy Morris. The Tigers finished the year 6-6-0 overall but were not ranked.

HERE COME THE TIGERS OF '78

By the third game, Central was ranked No. 3 by the *Arkansas Gazette* and No. 4 by the *Arkansas Democrat*. The opening game with the Forrest City Tigers was won 24-0 followed by an upset victory, 8-7, over the Pine Bluff Zebras.

The following three opponents were held to zero: Catholic High, 10-0, Shreveport, 17-0 and Hot Springs, 0-0. This team could not lose, bringing home a 27-6 win from West Memphis, a 23-6 victory over NLR Ole Main, a 14-14 tie with El Dorado, and a 13-7 NLR Northeast win. This was the year to travel to Fort Smith and Danny's grandparents, Mr. and Mrs. Joe Dickey, and relatives, Dorothy and Johnny Deaton, came to see him play. Danny's passing made up most of the yardage and we took home a 17-7 victory.

The next week at a packed Quigley Stadium, No. 2 Little Rock Central took on No. 1 Little Rock Parkview. This game ended in a 7-7 tie.

THANKSGIVING DAY GAME

The last game of the season was on Thanksgiving Day with Hall High and it was always a fierce battle with the stands packed.

"During the first 24 minutes, Central's defense allowed only one first down and 15 yards of total offense. An 11-yard run by Rodney Hayes, a 26-yard field goal by Roland Pennington, and a 52-yard pass from Danny

Nutt to Dunnick put the Tigers up 17-0 at half time. Hall High did fight back during that final half, but with an interception from Hall, Central ran out the clock. It was 17-14 victory.

"This was the second state title under Coach Cox and the second undefeated state championship team in four seasons at the school, which earned him the Arkansas High School Coach of the Year honor in 1978. Central was named State High School champions by the Associated Press." - *Tiger Pride*, by Brian Cox.

The turkey, dressing and pumpkin pies were definitely enjoyed by all on that Thanksgiving Day.

BASKETBALL

Immediately, after the football season was over, Danny joined the basketball team, and he played point guard, as mentioned before. Although it was a late start, very soon he would be in the starting lineup. There were many exciting basketball and football games during those three years!

In Danny's senior year, Dennis played on the team with Danny, although he was one year behind him. The Central High Tigers were state basketball champions and they were playing for the overall title. The game was played at the University of Central Arkansas in Conway. There was *"a packed house" and we were leading until the last three minutes. We lost that game by one point and, needless to say, we were heartsick! In spite of that game, Danny had a wonderful high-school career!

---

* a packed house – filled to capacity

Little Rock Central High School basketball

Danny, #9, quarterback for Little Rock Central High

COLLEGE/UCA

Danny began his college career on a football scholarship at the University of Central Arkansas in Conway, Ark. He played football on scholarship and basketball as a walk on.

The coach promised us, during recruiting, that Danny's friend, Roger, would be his roommate in the football dormitory even though he did not play football. When we arrived on campus, we were told he had not been assigned to room with Danny. If you know Houston Sr., we stayed there until Roger got re-assigned—it took awhile.

Danny was the quarterback for the UCA Bears for two years and then there was a coaching change. With the new coaching staff, Danny was listed as third-string quarterback. As you can imagine, Houston Sr. was not happy. "If you're going to sit on the bench," he said, "you sit on the bench at the best college you can find. You can be third-string quarterback at the University of Arkansas."

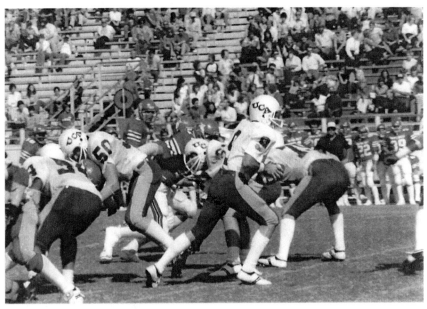

Danny, #9, quarterback for UCA

Danny, quarterback for University of Arkansas

UNIVERSITY OF ARKANSAS

Danny transferred to the University of Arkansas after his sophomore year. As he sat out his first year, he had the opportunity to observe coaching techniques under Coach Lou Holtz. After the 1983 season, Coach Holtz left Arkansas and Ken Hatfield, a Razorback standout in the '60s, returned to Fayetteville as head football coach.

In the fall of 1984, the quarterback, Brad Taylor, was injured and Danny became the starting quarterback for the Razorbacks. They were playing Navy at War Memorial Stadium in Little Rock, Ark. That was HUGE!!!

Danny played a near-flawless game. James Shibest, a receiver, who later was an assistant coach for Houston Dale for many years, caught every ball Danny threw and was named Most Valuable Player of the game. The Razorbacks won 33-10. They went to the Liberty Bowl two years in a row. Danny loved Ken Hatfield and enjoyed playing for him very much.

After graduating from the University of Arkansas, Danny became a graduate assistant and helped the Razorbacks to three-straight bowl appearances in 1986, 1987 and 1988.

COACHING

Danny's first full-time coaching job started as receivers' coach at Division I-AA Appalachian State in N. C. in 1988 and 1989. His second coaching job was much closer to home. He joined the staff at Arkansas Tech in Russellville, Ark., where he was the quarterback/running back/receiver coach from 1989-1992. It was a great coaching experience and Russellville was and is a great place to live.

DANNY JOINS BROTHER AT MURRAY STATE

In 1993, Danny joined his brother, Houston Dale, at Murray State in Ky. They took the team to the top, winning back-to-back championships 1995 and 1996.

His first full-time Division I-A job was Boise State in 1997. The families really enjoyed Idaho and loved snow skiing there. After turning the program around in one year, they were returning to their alma mater in Fayetteville.

RUNNING BACKS COACH/UNIVERSITY OF ARKANSAS

For nine seasons Danny performed his dream job as the running backs coach at the University of Arkansas. During those years, he had the good fortune of recruiting and mentoring outstanding players like Kenny Hamlin, Cedric Cobbs, Jonathan Luigs, Peyton Hillis, Jamaal Anderson, Felix Jones, Darren McFadden, and others.

In year 2002, Danny's running backs did not fumble one time during the regular season or during the Southeastern Conference game, which was a record. He received special recognition for this accomplishment from Coach Broyles.

Quarterbacks and running backs coach at Arkansas Tech

At Murray State with brother, Houston Dale

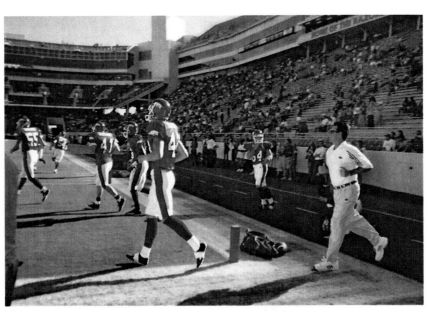

Running backs coach at University of Arkansas

THE SCARE OF OUR LIVES

At the end of the 1999 season, Danny and his running backs, along with the rest of the team, were preparing to go to the Citrus Bowl in Orlando, Fla, when a catastrophic crisis happened to our family! Danny was diagnosed with a brain-stem bleed—something you hope never happens to you!

Even now, to think about it gives me chills through and through. Up to this time, we didn't know much about the brain-stem. We learned that it is like a little cable system that controls just about every area of the human body. Never was Danny's determination more evident than when he underwent a delicate surgical procedure to stop the bleeding.

It has been said that neurosurgery is an art, and we were referred to the most talented, magnificent artist in the world, Dr. Gazi Yasargil, at UAMS in Little Rock, Ark. We are so grateful to him and know we were divinely placed in his hands. You would know him by his white doctor's coat, his thick eyebrows and his native Turkish accent.

John Tew Jr., M.D. and former student of Yasargil, wrote:

"In surgery, Dr. Yasargil needed no helper other than his wife, Dianne, who transferred instruments without verbal or visual communication in a symphony of motion that was punctuated by an occasional sigh of wonder from the audience."

Speaking in broken English with a strong Turkish accent, Dr. Yasargil explained: "As a doctor, I'm going to marry with each person or think my patients are my children. You cannot take a leaf from the tree. I like to see the entire tree. I like to see children around mother and father. It's very important to understand. I like to bring the people to the point that they know we are going together on a trip. It may end very "good," but it may end with a negative. They also are realizing they may die in my hands. I am well intended but it may go wrong. This knowing beforehand is scary."

Yes, we were all very scared—scared-to-death in fact. After about five apprehensive hours, surgery was over and all went well. Then we were on that arduous road to recovery!

Before Danny's illness, he was so healthy, active and strong. But now he could not walk or feed himself. He was 40 pounds lighter after his time in the hospital and surgery. He could not tolerate any noise, which meant his children could only visit for a brief time each day. The paralysis on the left side of his face kept the left eye from blinking; therefore, it would dry out and would have to be sewn shut from time to time. His eyes were so sensitive that we couldn't turn on any lights or television.

Many times even going to UAMS was too stressful for him and the doctors would come to our home. They were so wonderful to us!

Since he could hardly walk, we'd try to get him in the wheelchair. First, we would get him in a sitting position, take his blood pressure and heart rate, and then help him to a standing position, rechecking blood pressure and heart rate. At times the blood pressure would go over the top or it might bottom out. In either case, we would sit him back down and start all over at a later time. When we finally got to our destination, we would go through the same procedure to get him out of the wheelchair.

Gradually, we started walking him from the bedroom to his recliner. With me on one side and dad on the other, we'd start down the hall, resting in between. It was a "day's work," it seemed, to get from one place to another.

Danny's physical therapist was a godsend. She said that when someone has surgery like this, you never know what the motor skills will be like, but Danny had complete faith that he was going to be fine. She worked with him every day for three months.

The way he was making progress was indeed a miracle! Dr. Yasargil was so proud of his progress. He would just stare at Danny with arms folded, a big smile, and say over and over in his strong Turkish accent, *"You are Mi-rac-u-lous!"*

We understand why Dr. Yasargil was named "Neurosurgery's Man of the Century, 1950-1999" by *Neurosurgery,* the official journal of the Congress of Neurological Surgeons.

Dr. Yasargil designed the floating microscope, as well as many other instruments needed for brain-stem surgery.

Danny with Dr. Al-Mefty (center) and Dr. Yasargil on right

Danny deals with this catastrophe in a very positive manner. On our every inquiry about his well-being, his response never fails to be "Grrreat!"

After spending three full months with us in Little Rock, working diligently with his therapist, he was ready to go home with the promise that he would call home every day. That he did and, I might add, he still practices that habit.

As you can see, the road to recovery was a long and arduous one! Yes, indeed, we knew we had been on "a trip together," and we are so grateful to Dr. Yasargil and UAMS. We feel sure we could not have had better care anywhere in the world.

We are also grateful to all the people in the state of Arkansas and beyond, especially for prayers, cards and letters from people we didn't even know. Danny's story was printed in the *Dallas Morning News*. He received many calls and letters and was able to be an encouragement to many. One example was a 12-year-old boy, whose father, Jim Willcockson, Ph.D, Pain Management Center Manager in Nebraska Medical Center, wrote this letter to Coach Broyles:

"I emailed a friend on the Pig Pen Bulletin Board about Scott's condition. That friend then contacted another friend and he contacted Coach Danny Nutt. Within 48 hours, Coach Nutt called Scott in his hospital room. Scott was asleep so I talked to Coach Nutt. I can't tell you how much his kind words and his sincere interest meant to us at a time, when hope seemed like all we had.

"Coach Nutt called his office from Little Rock (despite having recruiting and game preparation duties to juggle) and had a Razorback cap mailed to Scott, which was already at our home on the day he was released from the hospital. I feel that both he and Houston have the kind of moral fiber and proper perspective on life that will always make us proud to have them as representatives of our beloved school. While I know that you appreciate what you have in HDN and Danny, I wanted to take this opportunity to share with you my perspective on what they mean to our team, our school and our state. I will never forget Coach Nutt's kindness, reassurance and support for my son in our time of crisis."

SECOND BLEED

In February 2000, at a time when we thought we were just about back to normal, the bleeding reoccurred. During the hospital stay, tests revealed a bleed but could not pinpoint it exactly, so an exploratory surgery was being considered. We were all at our *"lowest ebb." He thought he'd never be able to coach again. We

---

* lowest ebb – depressed, desperation

were all just devastated and horrified, because we knew what this surgery was like.

The night before the surgery was scheduled, we were all in the hospital room with Danny when Dr. Yasargil and Dr. Al-Mefty came in and announced—*"No Surgery!"* We all broke down and cried and cried! We were so grateful that we didn't have to go through a second surgery—not to mention the recovery. Danny could resume his coaching duties in a shorter time.

Houston Dale was so happy to have Danny back. He said, "I know he is my brother, but Danny is one of the best recruiters I've ever had. Coach Ken Turner was a great recruiter at Arkansas, because of all the All-American players he recruited and signed. You can say the same thing about Danny and his recruits: Kenny Hamlin, Jonathan Luigs, Peyton Hillis, Felix Jones, Jamaal Anderson, Darren McFadden and others."

He was loved by all especially by the mothers and grandmothers. Parents wanted to talk about their sons and he listened.

Danny was especially proud of Darren McFadden and Felix Jones, and he had this to say:

> "Darren McFadden was the first student athlete in the history of the school to win the Doak Walker Award twice, and the first student athlete from the University of Arkansas to go to New York, as a runner-up for the Heisman Trophy, two years in a row. He is also the best running back in America.
>
> "The privilege of coaching players like Darren McFadden and Felix Jones is a 'once-in-a-lifetime' experience!"

Danny's running backs helped Arkansas rank second in the Southeastern Conference and No. 22 in the nation by rushing for 187.4 yards per game.

Danny completed his ninth season as full-time assistant running backs coach for the Razorbacks before a change was inevitable.

OLE MISS

In 2007, the next coaching career step was as an Assistant Athletic Director for Player Development at Ole Miss. Houston Dale said, "Danny has a natural feel for the game, he is my sounding board, a trouble shooter, and very much involved with the players in the football operations at Ole Miss."

With 20 years of coaching experience, he developed a reputation as a hard worker both on the recruiting trail and on the practice field.

RUNNING BACKS COACH AT EASTERN ILLINOIS

Danny is now the running backs coach at Eastern Illinois University in Charleston, Illinois.

He is married to the former Carla Carlton, a graduate of the University of Central Arkansas. They have four daughters: Dallas, and triplets, Ashley, Brenna and Caylan.

Danny's family

DENNIS' EARLY YEARS

DENNIS

As the March winds blew, on March 25, 1963, a fourth son was born to the Nutt family. There were already three little boys, ages six, four and two.

My doctor squelched any idea of the possibility that it might be a girl. There was no ultrasound at that time, but my doctor knew by listening to the heart rate that it was a boy. He was always right. Sure enough at 6:42 p.m., weighing in at 7 lbs. and 1 oz. with light hair and blue eyes, a beautiful little boy was born and we were not disappointed. At this point, we thought we had to stick with the Ds, so we agreed on the name, Dennis Clay.

Houston Sr. was so excited to have four boys—he always said he wanted five boys. As time went by, his one-liner or wise-crack was, "If I had five boys, I'd have to have substitutes, so I'll settle for four."

When it was time to take Dennis home from the hospital, Danny, who was 22-months old, was not very happy to see either of us. I had been away in the hospital for seven days, but time heals everything. Very soon Danny was happy and became best buddies with his new baby brother.

Having four little boys, age six and under, was not as bad as people think. In fact it wasn't bad at all. On the contrary—it was wonderful! People often asked, "How many children do you have?" When I would say, "Four," invariably the response was, "Oh, no!" The wonderful thing is: they are never alone, they always have someone to play with, they are best friends and, besides, it's more economical. Just look at all the clothes that are handed down and the sleeping arrangement with all boys is much simpler. However, you won't sit down much!

My dear neighbor was in and out of our house daily. One day she convinced me I needed to sit for a moment and just enjoy the iced tea. As a rule, I would fix her iced tea and continue whatever I was doing. As the boys came in, one by one, from play to get a drink of water, they would notice I was sitting down and each one would ask the same question, "Mom, what's wrong?" By the time the fourth son had asked that same question, my neighbor was laughing, hilariously! She told everyone, "If Emmie ever sits down her boys think something is desperately wrong!"

Dennis enjoyed all the activity going on around him but enjoyed playing alone, too. He would play alone for hours with marbles, arranging them in different football formations and explain it to me.

He also loved listening to nursery rhymes and the Christmas records and, unlike his three older brothers, he always put the records back into their covers. One day Dennis was meticulously putting each record into its cover, as his older brothers looked on. One of them yelled, "Mom, come here! Dennis can read!" Of course, they knew he was too young to read, but Dennis explained that "Frosty the Snowman" had tiny, tiny snowflakes on the record and there would be something related to snow on the cover. This made it possible to match the records to their covers. Well, how about that? Amazing—and a great help for mom!

Dennis' best friends were Danny and his other brothers. He did not seem to have a special friend outside the family, but if Danny went to a friend's house usually Dennis was invited, too.

Being the fourth son, Dennis followed suit in doing whatever his brothers did, even if it was homework. After supper, the table was cleared and everyone gathered around the table to do homework. At that time Dennis did not have homework. He let me know he wanted to be seated at the table with his brothers, so every night I prepared homework for him. That habit must have carried over, because I never had to remind him to do his homework.

In no time Dennis was wearing a baseball uniform. He and Danny were batboys for their two older brothers' teams. Along with having fun, they were learning all the rules—how to be supportive, even how to "chatter" with the boys in the field and the best part was having a Coke after the game. That was a big treat because, as mentioned earlier, we didn't have Cokes at home.

At a very early age Dennis, too, was playing all kinds of ball. He, like his older brothers, was very fond of the deaf school gym and learned to dribble and shoot the ball very early. He, too, thought playing ball of any kind was just about the most important thing in life.

At one benefit game, during halftime, I was in the restroom and I heard applause. I thought, *"I'm missing the halftime entertainment."* Dennis was about three and he was out on the court, dribbling and shooting long shots. Of course, the audience was applauding after each basket he made. There was halftime entertainment all right and it was Dennis!

Dennis, like his older brothers, played in Little League baseball, YMCA football and Boys Club basketball and was on the Nutt Pee Wee basketball team.

His Pony League baseball team won the state tournament and played in the regional tournament in McAlester, Okla. The whole family went, including the grandparents, Mr. and Mrs. Joe Dickey, who lived in Oklahoma. Dennis was the pitcher. We had great games and a great time over the weekend, even though we didn't win the championship game.

YMCA football team Dennis (#10), assistant,
Danny (#15), and Houston Sr., coach

8-year-old Dennis on
YMCA football team

Dennis (quarterback) and
Coach Danny Black at
Forrest Heights Jr. High

LITTLE ROCK CENTRAL HIGH

The boys attended various elementary, middle and junior high schools but they all attended Little Rock Central High School. Each played quarterback on the football team and point guard on the basketball team.

Although Dennis was smaller than his three older brothers, he was also a Little Rock Central standout in basketball and football.

For seven straight years the Nutt boys had played point guard in basketball and quarterbacked the football team and now Dennis was about to make it eight.

He was Danny's back-up for two years, and he filled in for him only four times during those two seasons. He was the last Nutt brother to quarterback for the Central High Tigers. A familiar line we often heard was, "Are there any more Nutts to follow?"

In the *Central Pride*, Brian Cox wrote:

"Little Rock Central opened the new decade, 1980, as the *Arkansas Democrat's* No. 4 Team. The Tigers, who lost only one game during the 1979 season, returned only two starters from the previous season's dominating defense."

With nine wins, zero losses and two ties, only one more win was needed to claim their 18th state title under Coach Cox.

THANKSGIVING DAY GAME

The "Turkey Day" games were so exciting! Not only was it Thanksgiving Day but a football game, too! As usual, I started getting ready for that day, preparing food a week ahead. After the game, all the Fordyce folks would come home with us for Thanksgiving dinner. As said before, the outcome of the game largely determined the mood for the rest of Thanksgiving Day. We were all looking forward to our eighth traditional "Turkey Day" game and it was Dennis' time to quarterback the team.

For the first time in eight years, the ground was white with snow and ice and, of course, the weather was a key factor in the game. Dennis was in the shotgun formation for most of the game, because neither team could move the ball on the ground, as you can imagine. From the shotgun, Dennis did a good job passing the ball. Coach Cox said, "Dennis has the capability to throw the long ball as well as possessing the touch to drop the short pass in the flats."

Catching those passes for good yardage were Mark Horton, Olins and Byron Dunnick, and the final throw was to Fields for a 17-yard touchdown. The extra-point attempt was converted for a 7-0 lead and we hung on for three minutes and 26 seconds to win the game!

The victory provided Central High School with a share of the AAAAA Conference Championship and Central would remain Arkansas' No. 1 team. And you know we enjoyed the dinner and fellowship very much on that Thanksgiving Day!

The Thanksgiving Day games we remember so fondly are a thing of the past. The 1983 season brought an end to the AAAAA Conference as well as Little Rock Central's traditional Thanksgiving Day games.

From Brian Cox's *Tiger Pride*:

> "In 1934, a tradition began when Little Rock High School and North Little Rock High School agreed to schedule their game on the holiday. This series lasted 23 years before Little Rock Hall High School opened in 1958. With the opening of the new Little Rock school, Central began a new tradition by playing its cross-town rival on Thanksgiving Day."

BASKETBALL

Like his older brothers, as soon as the last football game was over on Thanksgiving Day, Dennis was in the gym. This was his first love. In no time at all he would be in the starting lineup, even though the basketball boys had been practicing since October.

In 1979 as a sophomore, Dennis was the leading scorer on the basketball team at Central. He lettered all three years and earned All-State honors in both football and basketball. He also made the All-Star squad.

Central's Dennis Nutt tries to shoot over Ole Main's Triplett.

1981 Tiger basketball

Dennis - an All-Star

Dennis in action as Tiger quarterback

END OF THE NUTT ERA

"The end of the 1980 season brought an end to the Nutt era. The starting quarterback position for Little Rock Central High School belonged to this family for eight consecutive years. Houston Dale (1973-1975), Dickey (1976), Danny (1977-1979) and Dennis (1980) combined to lead Central's football team to three state championships. All four received college scholarships for their athletic ability." - *Tiger Pride*, Brian Cox.

Little Rock Central High School

COLLEGE CAREER/TCU

Dennis turned down early scholarship offers from UALR and UCA, hoping for an opportunity to play in the Southwest Conference. He was so excited when the offer came to play for Coach Killingsworth at TCU. Houston Dale and Dickey had played for him when he was at OSU. It was farther away from home than I had hoped and, unlike his older brothers, he did not have a close friend as a roommate.

Dennis was our fourth son to earn a scholarship and he had an outstanding career at TCU. When he was a junior, he scored 36 points against Akeem Olajuwon's Houston Cougars, ranked No. 6, and made 32 points against an Arkansas Razorback team, ranked No. 7. Alvin Robertson and Joe Kleine played on this team.

Dennis averaged 17.8 points and was voted First Team All-Southwest Conference in 1984 and 1985. Later he was selected to the

All-Time Southwest Conference team. He ranked third nationally in free-throw shooting percentage. He scored 1,192 career points, which is still in the top 20 in TCU history. Dennis, a graduate of TCU, was inducted into the T.C.U. Hall of Fame for Basketball in October 2009.

Dennis said that, ever since the days he played in the backyard with his brothers, his dream was to make it in the NBA. They would watch an NBA game on television then run outside where the basketball goal was nailed to a tree and try all the moves.

"When I was at TCU, I started thinking I had a realistic chance at the NBA and when I wasn't drafted after my senior year, it was very upsetting. I looked back to my high school days and decided if I could prove people wrong then, I could prove them wrong again."

Dennis' jersey (#20), along with some "important" players' jerseys

TCU Lettermen's Association Hall of Fame logo

TCU players and Coach Killingsworth

Dennis playing for TCU

Dennis as a Maverick

PRO BASKETBALL

The chances of playing in the NBA are a million-to-one. One day that call came to join the Dallas Mavericks. Dickey said jokingly, "Dennis, I can't believe you're going to play for the Dallas Mavericks, I'm better than you!" This was a very exciting time for Dennis, living his dream. He couldn't believe it was real.

During his time with the Dallas Mavericks, they won the Mid-West Division. At that time they did not own their own plane. They flew commercial but always first class. Dennis scored his career high, 11 points, during a game against the Golden State Warriors.

Playing at home at the Reunion Arena was a great experience. As the game progressed, the home crowd would start chanting, louder and louder, "Nutt! Nutt! Nutt!" I don't know if it was the chanting but Coach Motta would put Dennis in the game.

Dennis said, "In the NBA, I had a chance to watch some great ones—Chris Mullin, Larry Bird, Michael Jordan—I saw those guys warm up and saw them work. They had the same pattern. I arrived at the arena at 5:30 p.m. for a 7:30 p.m. game against Bird's Boston Celtics. As I walked through the tunnel to the dressing room I heard a ball bouncing. I saw Larry Bird, dripping wet with sweat, and I asked the security guard what time Larry had arrived? He said, '4:30.'"

Dennis achieved his goal as an NBA basketball player because of his determination and hard work. He played six seasons in the NBA and semi-pro, which included NBA, CBA, La Crosse Catbirds, Sioux Falls Skyforce and one year in Real Madrid for George Karl in the European Basketball Association.

Houston Sr. and I had our passports ready to go to Spain, but a knee injury forced Dennis to return home sooner than planned. Houston and I missed seeing Spain and the bullfights. We couldn't believe it, but we were glad to get Dennis home!

Dennis is a perfect example of one who accomplished his life-long goal by believing in himself and working very hard. Dickey often uses Dennis' example as motivation for his teams, leading to this point:

You can do anything you want, if you are willing to work hard and never give up!

GRAD ASSISTANT/ASSISTANT COACH

Dennis worked one season as a graduate assistant at Texas A&M under Shelby Metcalf before a four-year stint as an assistant coach at West Ark Community College in Fort Smith, Arkansas. In 1992, they were champions in the B1 State East Conference.

Dickey and Dennis at ASU

ASU assistant coaches Tony Medlock, Charlie Fenske, and Dennis

During 1995-2000, Dennis had the opportunity to work for his brother, Dickey, at ASU as men's assistant basketball coach. They worked well together and this was a great time for mom and dad as well. We could see a game, two families, drive home and Houston Sr. could sleep in his own bed. At that time, all four boys were coaching in Arkansas. That was just grand and too good to last forever.

During Dennis' time at ASU, he had a part in taking the Indians to the NCAA. To get your team to the NCAA is a great accomplishment.

At times, he did shooting clinics for basketball camps, Boys Clubs in different cities, and even in Singapore, China. He would have half of the group keep up with every basket made and the other half keep up with baskets missed. He usually completed 92 to 96 shots out of 100 during his clinic performances. He wore a microphone explaining every move. He started out with lay-ups, moving out with each shot. He stressed a routine for shooting using proper form, and it was evident in his free-throw instruction—*bounce, bounce, bounce three times, shoot, swish!*

"It takes work, too." he would tell the campers, "If you want to be really good, you've got to spend a lot of time practicing. Get your dad or a brother to help rebound. It's hot outside, but that's no excuse to stay on the couch. You've got to get out there and work at it."

After Dennis had worked five years with his older brother, Dickey, he decided it was time to try for a head-coaching job. An interview was finally cleared at Southwest Texas State (now Texas State) in San Marcos. The hiring of the head coach was pretty much a done deal, but they agreed to do a courtesy interview.

He had his speech in order—with advice from his older brothers—and he was ready. Dressed in his Sunday best, he delivered his speech. The committee called an executive meeting. Lo and behold, this courtesy interview had turned into the real deal! The A. D. at Southwest Texas State called Coach Broyles and asked, "How is it to have a Nutt on your staff?" Coach Broyles responded, with his Georgia accent, *"Won-da-ful, Won-da-ful!"* The calls were going back and forth. Coach Broyles, very excited, called Houston Dale and said, *"Your bro-thur has turned the committee! Your bro-thur has turned the committee! He's gonna be the next head coach!"*

HEAD COACH

Dennis was hired as men's head basketball coach at Southwest Texas State, (now Texas State). The A. D. at that time was the late Coach Jim Wacker, the former football coach at TCU. He said, "I love someone that has zest and enthusiasm for life and he lights it up. He loves coaching, he loves young people and he has a great basketball background."

Coach Wacker's death on August 26, 2003 was a great loss to Dennis. He was 66 years old and he not only was Dennis' athletic director but mentor, friend and a father figure. All of his words were encouraging words and so supportive. He was a great man and is sorely missed!

When Dennis took over the Southwest Texas State Bobcats in 2000, they were picked last or next to last in the Southland Conference race. He led the team to a 13-15 finish and a 10-10 mark in the conference.

Southwest Texas State was seventh in the league standings but just one win from a third-place finish. Dennis spent six years as men's head basketball coach at Texas State. In 2003, Southwest Texas State became Texas State.

Ed Teeter, a retired coach living in San Marcos and a big fan of the San Marcos Bobcats, wrote this note to Houston Sr.:

"Houston,

"The Southwest Texas Basketball continues to improve. They are well coached, very competitive and will beat you in the last quarter or 10 minutes in the last half. I think Dennis is an outstanding coach. He handles his boys real well. You can tell this in his time-outs. He coaches and tells them what to do rather than as some coaches do—raise h*** with them the entire time-out. He will have a good career as a college basketball coach.

"I know you are proud of all your sons. They are fine men.

"Best Wishes,
"Ed Teeter, 'old coach'"

Dennis resigned from Texas State after the 2007 season. The next stop was Myrtle Beach, South Carolina.

Dennis as Head Coach at Texas State

COASTAL SOUTH CAROLINA

Dennis took an assistant coaching job at Coastal South Carolina University in Myrtle Beach, S. C. After one year, Buzz Peterson, the head coach, took Dennis with him as a Pro Scout.

PRO SCOUT

In the fall of 2007, Dennis began a new career as a Pro Scout for Michael Jordan's Charlotte Bobcats. Even though he enjoyed watching games and visiting with coaches, he missed coaching.

OUACHITA BAPTIST UNIVERSITY

I do believe that through divine intervention Dennis became the head basketball coach at Ouachita Baptist University in Arkadelphia, Arkansas on June 1, 2011. He said, "It is a joy to coach at Ouachita. I am able to relax and coach without pressure, and the greatest thing of all is to have the support of my athletic director, David Sharp, and our president, Dr. Rex Horne."

Dennis is married to the former Vicki Hughes, a graduate of TCU and a cheerleader for the Horned Frogs. They have twin daughters, Myca and Macy, who now attend Ouachita Baptist University and live on campus. They consider this a gift from God. Dennis and Vicki reside in Arkadelphia.

Dennis' family

Houston Sr. and four boys

ALL FOUR FOLLOWED IN DAD'S FOOTSTEPS

As the boys started their coaching careers, I was often asked this question: "How is it that all four sons have followed in their father's footsteps?" It made me think, "*Was it environment, mentors, or was it the genes?*"

All four boys lived at the same place, at 311 Rice Street, which was two and a half blocks from the deaf school. All were born there except Houston Dale, who was 18 months old when we moved there. Our work was all about games and we didn't have vacations, because we played ball all summer. Some might say our life was simple—revolving around school, church and games.

I remember the boys' love and dedication for their games. I also knew their father expected their best at every outing. Houston had a huge influence on his sons; however, I was taken aback when I read an essay Dennis wrote in his high school English class. The following is an excerpt from that essay:

> "My oldest brother, Houston Dale, was the perfect older brother who seemed to do everything right. He set the bar very high and my other brothers, Dickey,

Danny, and myself did our very best to be as good as he was, not only in sports but in everything. When something came along and we had to make a decision, the first thing we thought about was, "What would Houston Dale think about that?"

Before reading Dennis' essay, I never thought about the influence of siblings, WOW! Whatever the motivation, we were very proud of each one and the commitment to the hard work that is required to earn an athletic scholarship, as well as being good citizens.

Whatever shapes lives—environment, parents, genes or siblings— *"Sons are a heritage from the Lord...like arrows in the hands of a warrior...blessed is the man whose quiver is full of them"* (Psalms 127:3-5 – NIV).

Yes, we are truly blessed that all four sons chose to follow in their father's footsteps. Although our sons coach at the college level and their father coached at the high school level, the long hours and hard work are the same.

Houston Sr. would be proud that his sons are carrying on his legacy.

Epilogue

This story is about a little boy who had a dream. It was during the Great Depression that a legend was born to deaf parents in a modest, unpainted frame home in Dallas County, Fordyce, Ark.

> *"Before I formed you in the womb I knew you, before you were born I set you apart; I appointed you as a prophet to the nation"* (Jeremiah 1:5 – NIV).

As his life unfolded, you can see the plan God had for him, working with the deaf to encourage them to work hard, never give up, and achieve his or her goal.

Making this dream possible, he was gifted in athletics with a passion for basketball. To help him accomplish his dream, coincidently, or with God's divine intervention, he was led to the college library at OSU, where he met his wife and helpmate, who joined him on his mission.

He not only worked with the deaf but juggled two worlds, making people feel special by using his favorite phrase, *"You're the best!"*

To carry on his legacy are four sons, who are following in his footsteps.

It is my prayer that this story was a blessing to you and that Houston's dream has been accomplished—that *"life is better for deaf people"* and that you, too, may accomplish your dream!

Remember, *"With man this is impossible, but with God all things are possible"* (Matthew 19:26 – NIV).

THANK YOU!
Drawing by Myca Nutt, granddaughter

APPENDIX 1:
REASONABLE TAX

A. Reasonable Tax: With passage of the Hall Net Income Tax Law in February 1929, a reasonable tax was placed on all net incomes. With funds from this "reasonable tax" a new school for deaf children in Little Rock was completed, along with a new hospital for the mentally ill near Benton, Arkansas, and additional buildings for the Arkansas Tuberculosis Sanitarium at Booneville, Arkansas. - Information from *"Governors of Arkansas"* by Donovan, Gatewood Jr., and Whayne, pp. 177-179.

B. Governor's Favorite Project: The school was named for Governor Parnell. Parnell Hall is a two-story structure, with classrooms, office space, restrooms on the first floor. There is a short flight of steps down to the auditorium and gymnasium. Additional classrooms are on the second floor.

The original light fixtures are still in the entrance of Parnell Hall and hanging on the spacious wall on the right is a huge picture of the beautiful, late Mrs. Riggs, who was superintendent at the school during the 30s.

The gymnasium had wood flooring and built-in wooden platforms for seating, which was later replaced with concrete slabs, where seats with backs were placed. They have since been replaced. The dressing rooms and trophy cases were added later.

The auditorium at the school was named, Parnell Hall for the governor whose "tax program" helped build it.

APPENDIX 2:
"THE BEAR"

"Bear Bryant was born in Moro Bottom, near Fordyce, Arkansas in 1913 and grew up there. He was the eleventh of 13 children. He got his nickname, "Bear," when he wrestled a bear on the stage of the local theater.

"He was a star on the Fordyce High School *Redbugs* football team and was good enough to get a football scholarship to the University of Alabama.

"Bear Bryant was head coach at Alabama from 1958 to December 15, 1982. He took his Alabama Crimson Tide teams to six national championships.

"Without a doubt, he gives his mother credit for his success. He died January 26, 1983." - *The Last Coach: A Life of Paul "Bear" Bryant* - (inside cover).

APPENDIX 3:
SAMUEL FORDYCE

"The town was named for Samuel Fordyce, who enlisted and fought in the Civil War. He quickly rose to officer status, and participated in the battles of Chickamauga and Shiloh, among others.

"He spearheaded efforts in building thousands of miles of railroads in the South and Southwest during the nineteenth century, including the Cotton Belt route that crossed Arkansas and Dallas County.

"Samuel Fordyce also recognized the possibilities in Hot Springs, as a Health Resort and turned those possibilities into reality. Bathhouse Row, which includes Fordyce Bathhouse, remains one of the most elegant structures of its kind anywhere in the world. Samuel Fordyce was an extraordinary man. Fordyce was a trade center for a fertile five-county area, a town closer to being self-sufficient than many towns in the Deep South, making it a better place than most in which to weather the Depression." - *The Last Coach: A Life of Paul "Bear" Bryant.*

"The Fordyce Lumber Co. was established in the late 1880s. More than a fourth of the city's working population was employed by the company.

"Georgia-Pacific purchased Fordyce Lumber in 1963 and opened its Southern pine plywood plant the following year.

"The sad news came in early December 2009, Georgia-Pacific Corp. officials told employees of the plywood plant that it would close permanently, leaving 340 Arkansans out of work." - *Democrat-Gazette* - Rex Nelson - 1-16-2010.

APPENDIX 4:
FORDYCE

"Fordyce had the proudest high school football tradition in the state, if not the entire South. In fact, the first high school football team in Arkansas was organized there in 1904. The program was built by a former New Yorker named Tom Meddick, who brought with him to Fordyce—in the words of J. Willard Clary—'a queer-shaped ball filled with air that had a crazy way of bouncing.' (J. Willard Clary was the Fordyce correspondent for the *Arkansas Gazette* and the grandson of the founder of the Clary Training School.)

"In 1908, this local Fordyce team traveled to the state capital for a game against Little Rock High School. The visitors lost 13-0 but gave a fine display of courage against a team that had 'twenty times the manpower to draw upon.'

"The crowd was estimated to be four hundred, which many thought was the largest number to see a football game in Arkansas up to that time.

"In 1909, Clary got its first crosstown rival when Fordyce fielded its first team. The two-year rivalry culminated in a match between the two unbeaten teams on Thanksgiving Day in 1911.

"Clary whipped Fordyce, 39-0. Shortly afterward, Clary closed its doors, and the faculty and students moved to Fordyce High." - *The Last Coach: A Life of Paul "Bear" Bryant,* by Allen Barra, pp. 27-28.

APPENDIX 5:
GREAT-GRANDFATHER

"Houston Sr.'s great-grandfather, Benjamin Franklin Nutt, born 1824 in Alabama, migrated with his family to Calhoun County, Arkansas, the county just below Dallas County. Benjamin was married to Judith Joana Eagle and the couple had five children. She died giving birth to triplets in 1860. The triplets also died at birth.

"According to the records, Benjamin was a very large man, a true frontiersman, loved nature, the out-of-doors, and always respected the rights of others.

"Many of Benjamin's brothers and cousins were forcefully pressed into the Confederate army. The state of Arkansas was divided into pro-slavery and anti-slavery. Benjamin was opposed to slavery and he went into hiding.

"In 1863, Benjamin's brother, Martin, died of typhoid fever while home on leave from the army. Benjamin came to the house to pay his respects, and to see his son who was sick as well. An outlaw group of Confederates called "Grey Backs" pursued Benjamin. The dogs picked up his scent and he had to run out the back door and across the field. As the family watched, the Grey Backs caught Benjamin. They hanged him.

"The family learned about his death from a black man. They took the body down and buried him near the site of his death, covering the grave with rocks and stones.

"Benjamin's death left his five children orphans. They had only hominy and milk to eat. Finally, Benjamin's brother, John Nutt, arrived on leave from the army and took the children to his wife,

Josephine, who had moved to Kentucky for the duration of the war. Josephine was also a sister to the children's mother. John and Josephine raised Benjamin's children, returning to Arkansas when the war ended.

"The hanging took place in April or early May of 1863, southeast of Fordyce." - Excerpt from *Making Tracks*, by Lee Ann Smith-Trafzer, pp. 90-92.

APPENDIX 6:
VOCATIONAL TRAINING FOR THE DEAF

"The young men who attended the deaf school learned the trade of shoe repair and did very well. The young ladies were instructed in sewing and housekeeping.

"Training along vocational lines has always been given a prominent part in state-supported schools for deaf children. In 1874, shoe making and repairing, with H. J. Jernigan as instructor, was commenced and this vocation has proved a fortunate field for the deaf of Arkansas. In 1934, numerous shoe shops were operated by deaf men, who learned the trade at the state school." -*A Brief History of the Education of the Deaf in the State of Arkansas,* pp 10-11.

APPENDIX 7:
MARTHA'S VINEYARD

AN ISOLATED ISLAND OFF THE MASSACHUSETTS COAST

From the 17th Century, Martha's Vineyard had an extremely high rate of hereditary deafness among its residents. The deaf people communicated by using sign language. It was called Martha's Vineyard Sign Language (MVSL). This language later merged with mainland signs to form American Sign Language.

As the deaf children at the Vineyard started attending schools and marrying mates from the mainland, gradually the deaf Vineyard population died out. Statistics show the last deaf Vineyard native passed away in the 1950s.

APPENDIX 8:
HISTORICAL HEROES IN DEAF EDUCATION

- Abbe Charles de l'Epée, (1712-1789), a French priest in the late 1760s, was one of the early educators of the deaf in France. He founded the first free school for deaf in Paris, France, in 1775. Epée, a distinguished educator of the deaf, allowed his methods in teaching the deaf to be available to the public and other educators. As a result of his openness, his methods became so influential that his mark is still apparent in Deaf Education today. He established teacher-training programs for foreigners who would take his methods back to their countries and establish schools for the deaf.
- Abbe Sicard, (1742-1822), a pupil, teacher and successor of the Epée School, wrote the first dictionary of signs, *Theorie DES SIGNES*.
- Laurent Clerc, (1785-1869), was born and raised in France. A student and teacher of the now-famous Epée School came to America with Gallaudet. Together they founded the first deaf school.
- Thomas Hopkins Gallaudet, (1787-1851), a hearing man and a minister, with Clerc's help, founded the first school, the American School for the Deaf at Hartford, Connecticut in 1817.
- By school year 1821-1822, the American School in Hartford had become a parent school for four such schools—the New York, Pennsylvania, Kentucky, and Ohio schools for the deaf. The Hartford school was not the only parent school, thus, sooner or later a school for the deaf was provided in each state.

- Edward Miner Gallaudet, (1837-1917) – The eighth and youngest child of Thomas and Sophia Gallaudet carried out his father's dream, which was higher education for the deaf. A bill was signed by President Lincoln. This was in the year of 1864.

This statue was unveiled on June 26, 1889. Thomas Gallaudet is seated in an old fashion three cornered chair, nine-year-old Alice Cogswell standing by his side, with his right hand in the form of an A, using the manual alphabet.

Friend/Teacher/Benefactor

APPENDIX 9:
FORDYCE BASKETBALL 1949-50

LINE UP

Helena	TP	Fordyce	TP
Mabry, forward	16	F. Nutt, forward	18
Whitworth, forward	8	H. Nutt, forward	14
Webster, center	6	Fielder, center	3
Harness, guard	4	Gray, guard	2
Proctor, guard	10	Lynn, guard	1
Joyner, forward	0	McRee, forward	0

Officials: Pryor Evans and Ebb Pickens

APPENDIX 10:
LEGENDARY COACHES

ADOLPH RUPP – SEPTEMBER 2, 1901- DECEMBER 10, 1977

The first legendary coach Houston Sr. played for was Adolph Rupp, at the University of Kentucky, 1951-1953.

Several nicknames are associated with him, such as, the "Baron of Bluegrass," because he took more than 80 percent of his players from the state of Kentucky and turned them into champions.

Colorful as he was successful, sportswriters throughout the nation tagged Rupp with another descriptive title, "The Man in the Brown Suit," because of his preference of brown as his game-night wardrobe.

Coach Rupp's achievements were endless. In 1944 he was recognized for the highest individual coaching achievement in basketball by being elected to the Helms Foundation Hall of Fame and basketball Hall of Fame in Springfield, Mass. In 1945, Rupp was named to the Kentucky Hall of Fame as the second man to be so honored in the history of the state and there were many other achievements.

From his arrival in Lexington in 1930 to his last game in 1972, Rupp accumulated 879 wins, captured 27 Southeastern Conference titles and led the Kentucky Wildcats to four national championships. Rupp's players and assistant coaches say he was a strict disciplinarian whose practices were akin to military drills and a man who wouldn't put up with disobedience on any level.

Adolph Rupp spent the first years of his life in poverty but he found an outlet in the game of basketball. With his achievements in high school, coupled with his strict discipline and a devotion to the academics of his players, he earned the head-coaching job at UK in 1930.

Coach Rupp died December 10, 1977.

HENRY "HANK" IBA –AUGUST 6, 1904 - JANUARY 15, 1993

The second legendary coach Houston played for was Coach Henry "Hank" Iba, Oklahoma A&M. (1953-1956.)

"Iba was born and raised in Easton Missouri. He played college ball at Westminster College, Fulton, Missouri. As a collegiate coach at Oklahoma A&M, later known as Oklahoma State and three-time mentor of US Olympic teams, Iba did more than win national championships and bring home gold medals. He transcended greatness. His teams were methodical, ball-controlling units that featured weaving patterns and low scoring games.

To name a few distinctions, he was elected to the Oklahoma Sports Hall of Fame, the Oklahoma Hall of Fame, the Missouri Hall of Fame, the Helms Foundation All-Time Hall of Fame for basketball and Naismith Memorial Basketball Hall of Fame at Springfield, Mass. Henry Iba is thought to be one of the toughest coaches in NCAA history.

Coach Henry Iba died on January 15, 1993, in Stillwater, Okla.

APPENDIX 11:
THE OUTLOOK FOR 1951-52

UNIVERSITY OF KENTUCKY

"The defending national collegiate titlist, who gave the nation's cage teams a new mark at which to shoot by becoming the first three-time tournament winner in NCAA history last March, will present a balanced roster listing four seniors, three juniors, four sophomores and ten freshmen.

"Seniors: Bill Spivey, Shelby Linville, Lucian Whitaker, Bobby Watson.

"Juniors: Frank Ramsey, Cliff Hagan, Lou Tsioropoulos.

"Sophomores: Bill Evans, Gayle Rose, Gene Neff, Willie Rouse.

"Freshman: George Cooke, James Flynn, Houston Nutt, Ronald Clark, Dan Swartz, Neale Cosby, Charles Keller, Woodrow Preston, Brown Sharpe, Cliff Dwyer.

"Kentucky will be without its All-American center, seven foot Bill Spivy, for at least the first month of the season and possibly for the entire campaign. The Georgia Pine most valuable cage player in the nation last year and number one man on everybody's "all" teams, injured a knee, and had surgery for a torn cartilage.

"Still on crutches and unable to put any appreciable weight on the knee at season's start, Spivey posed Coach Rupp the biggest problem in 1951-52 plans.

"The Wildcats, with 13 native Kentuckians on the roster of 21 players, open the season Dec. 8 against Washington & Lee and then take on Xavier, Minnesota, St. John's, DePaul and UCLA in that order before winding up their December engagements in the Sugar Bowl Tournament with St. Louis U., Brigham Young, and Villanova.

"The bulk of the January-February schedule consists of competition with conference foes as Kentucky seeks its ninth consecutive Southeastern Conference title. Only non-conference tilts slated in the New Year are with powerful Notre Dame, DePaul and Xavier.

"The rest of the Wildcat lineup shapes up about as expected with Shelby Linville, 6' 5" senior from Middletown, Ohio, and Frank Ramsey, 6' 3" junior from Madisonville, Ky., as probable forwards; and Bobby Watson, 5' 10 1/2" senior from Owensboro, Ky., and Skippy Whitaker, 6' senior from Louisville, Ky., at guards.

"We will also be counting on one experienced reserve, Lou Tsioropoulos, 6' 5" junior forward-center." – Basketball Facts – *For Press and Radio*, Edited by Ken Kuhn, Sports Publicity Editor.

APPENDIX 12:
A BIT OF HISTORY

"The school's journey to 2400 West Markham was not an easy one. About the year 1850, the first class in Arkansas for 'deaf mutes,' as deaf children were called, was taught by J.W. Woodward in Clarksville, Arkansas. Due to insufficient funds, the school was closed.

"In 1867 Joseph Mount, a deaf man who had received instruction at the Pennsylvania School for the Deaf opened a school for deaf children in Little Rock. In 1868 the struggling school was taken over as a state institution. The school was given the title of 'The Arkansas Deaf Mute Institute.' Two tracts of land were donated. The latter tract is the present beautiful location of the Arkansas School for the Deaf.

"At the time of the grant the land was valued at $1.25 per acre. A rocky trail led through the hills to the site and wild turkeys abounded. The residential section of the city of Little Rock expanded its direction and in 1934 the land was worth more than half a million dollars.

"Even when the school was 26 years old, it was quite isolated. The road was very rough and at times almost impassable. By 1898 something was finally done and a carriage made its way to the city daily. The lady teachers took turns going to town once a week." – *A Brief History of the Education of the Deaf in the State of Arkansas*, by Beth Michaels Riggs, Superintendent, Arkansas School for the Deaf.

TWO GREAT EVENTS

In 1895 Dr. Alexander Graham Bell, who invented the telephone, visited the school.

In 1899 a disastrous fire destroyed the Administration Building at ASD.

"What was once the handsomest view in the State of Arkansas was a desolate scene of ruin when the sun rose yesterday morning. The fire, which broke out at 2 a.m. at the Deaf-Mute Institute, September 30th, burned itself out by 5 a.m., after destroying everything within reach. It was a number of years before the permanent buildings were completed to replace those that were destroyed by fire." -*Arkansas Gazette*, October 1, 1899.

Administration Building destroyed by fire at ASD

APPENDIX 13:
COACHES WINNING 20 GAMES OR MORE

Year	W-L	COACH
1928	24-6	Earl Bell
1939	27-6	Clyde Van Cleve
1940	23-8	Clyde Van Cleve
1941	26-0	Clyde Van Cleve
1948	25-2	Edward G. Foltz
1949	24-1	Edward G. Foltz
1951	25-3	Pearl Dunn
1952	20-7	Pearl Dunn
1968	24-9	Houston Nutt
1969	23-4	Houston Nutt
1970	26-4	Houston Nutt
1971	20-13	Houston Nutt

The National Deaf Prep Basketball Coach of the year 1949 was Edward S. Foltz and 1969 Houston Nutt. ASD has claimed six National Deaf Pre-Basketball Championships: 1928, 1939, 1941, 1948, 1949, and 1968. ASD is the first team to win back-to-back National Titles in 1948 and 1949.

APPENDIX 14:
BENNIE FULLER'S HIGH SCHOOL STATISTICS

- Freshman year, 1967-1968 - Total number of points for the year was 606. His highest number of points in one game was 43 and his point average was 22.8.
- Sophomore year, 1968-1969 - Total number of points for the year was 1,007. His highest number of points in one game was 52 and his point average was 35.9.
- Junior year, 1969-1970 - Total number of points for the year was 1,301. His highest number of points in one game was 98, and his point average was 44.9.
- Senior year, 1970-1971 - Total number of points for the year was 1,347.

His highest number of points in one game was 102, and his point average was 53.8.

ARKANSAS ACTIVITIES ASSOCIATION - 1999 INDUCTION GREAT MOMENTS IN HIGH SCHOOL SPORTS

- Most Points scored, Game:
- 103 - Dickie Pitts –(Wimauma, FL), 2-14, 1956
- 102 - Bennie Fuller – (Little Rock Arkansas School for the Deaf, AR), 12-4, 1971
- 102 - Ed Vondra – (Brainard NE), 1922
- 100 - Dajuan Wagner – (Camden, NJ), 1-16, 2001
- 100 - Greg Procell – (Noble Ebarb, LA), 1-29, 1970
- 100 - Tigran Grigorian – (Pico Rivera Mesroblan, CA) 2003.

APPENDIX 15:
A HOUSE RESOLUTION

The Resolution, introduced in the House of Representatives February 2, 1971 in honor of Bennie Fuller, commending him for his outstanding sportsmanship and scoring record as a member of the Arkansas School for the Deaf basketball team:

WHEREAS, the Arkansas School for the Deaf basketball team, the "Leopards," has compiled an outstanding season's record; and

WHEREAS, the "Leopards," coached by Mr. Houston Nutt, have benefited greatly by the remarkable performances by Bennie Fuller; and

WHEREAS, Bennie Fuller's 53.8 scoring average is the nation's highest among high school basketball players; and

WHEREAS, Bennie Fuller is the second highest all-time point maker in prep school history; and

WHEREAS, Bennie Fuller holds the all-time school records for the most points scored in one season (1,347), most points scored in one game (102), and highest average in a single season (53.8), even though these statistics are based on an incomplete season; and

WHEREAS, the accomplishments of Bennie Fuller, the "Leopard" team, and the coaching staff have brought distinction to the Arkansas School for the Deaf and the State of Arkansas,

NOW THEREFORE, BE IT RESOLVED BY THE HOUSE OF REPRESENTATIVES OF THE SIXTY-EIGHTH GENERAL ASSEMBLY OF THE STATE OF ARKANSAS:

That the House of Representatives hereby commends and congratulates Bennie Fuller for his outstanding sportsmanship and athletic ability displayed as a member of the Arkansas School for the Deaf basketball team, the "Leopards."

BE IT FURTHER RESOLVED that an appropriate copy of his Resolution shall be furnished by the Chief Clerk of the House of Representatives to Mr. Bennie Fuller.

Jim Linder, Representative

CPSIA information can be obtained at www.ICGtesting.com
Printed in the USA
LVOW11s1352200215

427719LV00001BA/87/P